A Passionate Engagement

A Memoir

by Ken Harvey

B
Harvey, K.

Harvey

A Passionate Engagement: A Memoir
by Ken Harvey

ISBN 978-1-929355-68-6
Library of Congress Control Number: 2010905798
Design and Cover by Laura Tolkow, Flush Left

Pleasure Boat Studio (and Aequitas Books) is a proud subscriber to the Green Press Initiative. This program encourages the use of 100% post-consumer recycled paper with environmentally friendly inks for all printing projects in an effort to reduce the book industry's economic and social impact. With the cooperation of our printing company, we are pleased to offer this book as a Green Press book.

Aequitas Books is an imprint of Pleasure Boat Studio: A Literary Press
Our books are available through the following:
SPD (Small Press Distribution) Tel. 800-869-7553, Fax 510-524-0852
Partners/West Tel. 425-227-8486, Fax 425-204-2448
Baker & Taylor 800-775-1100, Fax 800-775-7480
Ingram Tel 615-793-5000, Fax 615-287-5429
Amazon.com and **bn.com**

and through
PLEASURE BOAT STUDIO: A LITERARY PRESS
www.pleasureboatstudio.com
201 West 89th Street
New York, NY 10024

Contact **Jack Estes**
Fax; 888-810-5308
Email: pleasboat@nyc.rr.com

When an individual is protesting society's refusal to acknowledge his dignity as a human being, his very act of protest confers dignity upon him.

Bayard Rustin

The history of every country begins in the heart of a man or a woman.

Willa Cather

for B, E and S

I have changed many names in the writing of this book in order to protect people's privacy. Some non-essential details of people in the memoir have also been changed for the same reason. Conversations and details have been reconstructed to the best of my ability, although time and forgetfulness dictate that I have sometimes written keeping the spirit rather than the letter of people's words in mind.

CHAPTER ONE

ORIGINS

You can make history any number of ways. You can land on the moon. Discover a vaccination for polio. Hit more homeruns than anyone else in baseball. Build the first automobile.

Or you can simply ask to be married.

On March 26th, 2001, Heidi Norton and Gina Smith arrived at the City Clerk's office in Northampton, Massachusetts, to request a marriage license. They had been a couple for eleven years and purchased a home together. Heidi had borne their two sons. They had given the children the last name "Nortonsmith," combining their surnames, to emphasize the relationship between the two boys. Now Heidi and Gina wanted their relationship recognized by the law.

At first, the City Clerk assumed that Heidi was requesting the license for herself and her male fiancé who hadn't accompanied her to the Town Hall. When Heidi explained that the license was for the two women, the City Clerk politely denied their request. Same-sex marriage was not allowed in Massachusetts, she explained. The two women left empty-handed.

I can tell you exactly where I was when I heard most of the breaking news about the gay marriage debate —in the car, in my classroom, at the Massachusetts State House— but the day these two women applied for a marriage license remains elusive. Even when I did hear the news, it's likely I didn't grasp its significance. I was too jaded to imagine that getting married would be a possibility in my lifetime, so the day slipped by me.

My attitude would change. Within the next few years I would be protesting, writing letters, sending emails, and campaigning for politicians who supported my right to marry. I would become engaged in a civil rights movement that I hadn't even heard of growing up. I didn't learn about the Stonewall Riots – often cited as the beginning of the modern gay rights movement – until I was in college, at least ten years after that June weekend in 1969. But I have no reference point, no recollection of the who and the where and the when of hearing the word. I can only assume where I was during Stonewall, because summer weekends for us tended to follow the same routine.

Almost every Sunday from June to August, my mother took my sister and me to the beach while my father golfed. We'd load up the car with sandwiches, bags of potato chips, thermoses of Kool-Aid, beach blankets, collapsible chaise lounges, suntan lotion, and a transistor radio. We'd head toward the beach via the Causeway, the legendary connector between Lynn and Nahant where drag races like the one in the climactic scene in *American Graffiti* took place and young people were occasionally killed.

I never quite understood the appeal of having to pick out sand from sandwiches when you could just as easily have them at home, but then again I never was much of an outdoorsman. I left Boy Scouts the day after we held a "mock camping trip" and were asked to bring to a meeting what we would need for a weekend in the woods. I showed up with a book and a flashlight. No food. No Band-Aids. No sleeping bag. No extra clothes. Not even an extra set of underwear.

So the beach wasn't where I would have chosen to spend those weekends in the summer, but I made the most of it. I learned to enjoy eavesdropping on my mother and her friend, Lena, who often went with us. I read and listened to American Top Forty on the radio. I watched the shirtless men with their bronzed bodies.

I didn't recognize my attraction to those men as sexual at the time. At first I felt just a little more curious than I did when my mother took off her shorts and top to reveal her jet-black bathing suit. But one day my mother let me walk to the far end of the beach, at the Nahant-Lynn line, to the refreshment stand. Next to it was a bathroom and locker room where the lifeguards dressed and showered at the end of their duty.

When I entered the building, I expected some urinals, stalls, and perhaps a sink or two. But as I turned the corner, I saw three young men standing naked in the shower room. It was the first time I'd ever seen a naked man. My heart raced. I knew I shouldn't stare, but I couldn't help it. Their backsides were blinding white against the deep tan on their backs and legs. I became anxious and tried to turn away, but couldn't find the willpower. I watched one of the lifeguards wring out his orange swim trunks. I was stunned by the hair that fanned out from the base of his penis; no one had ever told me hair grew there. For a moment my whole body seemed so overwhelmed with feeling that I thought I might burst into tears. Finally the lifeguard looked at me, a wave of disgust crossing his face, and I knew I needed to go.

When I went to the urinal, I realized I was hard. I peed, urine splashing against my legs in two or three different streams. I had no idea what any of this meant, but I knew that whatever I was feeling, whatever had caused me to harden this way, was very wrong.

Seeing the naked men in the locker room was not the first time I felt profoundly different, profoundly *wrong*, even though it might be my earliest recollection that this difference was deeply sexual in nature. The feeling of being on the periphery goes back to my very first day of school in the early sixties.

I never went to kindergarten, so my earliest experience in a classroom – save for daily viewings of *Romper Room* – was at the Edward J. Sisson Elementary School in Lynn, a city famous for its shoe factories and the jingle, "Lynn, Lynn, the city of sin, you never come out the way you come in." My elementary school introduced me to the world of Dick and Jane. To American flags hung beside chalkboards and teachers, all women, whose names began with either Miss or Mrs. No *Ms.* No slacks for women, either. All the girls and teachers wore skirts and dresses.

On this first day I am wearing the white shirt my mother has washed and ironed, just as I will wear white shirts for the rest of the year. The wooden desks are lined up in five rows and for today, at least, I sit near the front, the *H* in Harvey falling on the second seat, second row. I can write my name, say the alphabet, but not much more. Mrs. O'Connor, a middle-aged woman with frosted hair, asks us to come up by row to sit in a semicircle of wooden chairs where she flashes phonics sounds printed in black magic marker on oak tag strips. I am told I am in the Blue Group.

There are things I don't get. When Mrs. O'Connor tells us it is time to go to the lavatory, I picture a science lab with test tubes. I don't really know what recess is, just that my mother has packed me a Devil Dog for it. But when *is* recess? Will Mrs. O'Connor tell us or are we simply expected to know? Finally she asks us to line up in front of the classroom and walks us to a large hot-topped yard surrounded by a chain link fence. There is a monstrous tree in the corner whose roots have cracked the pavement.

Mrs. O'Connor gathers us to explain the rules. Is *this* when I eat my Devil Dog? I take it out of the wrapper and cram it into my mouth. Some kids look at me. Why isn't anybody else eating? *Aghh.* I have whipped cream all over my face. My hands are sticky and I don't know what to do with the wrapper.

I've missed the explanation of the rules. Two girls begin to swing a jump rope. It swishes through the air and snaps against the ground. Other girls line up to break in and jump.

> *I know a little miss*
> *A pretty little miss*
> *Her name is Mississippi*
> *And she spells it like this:*
> *Capital M-I-S-S-I-S-S-I-P-P-I.*

"The boys are over there," Mrs. O'Connor says, pointing me toward the other end of the yard where they are running with a red dodge ball. I have no idea what they are doing. Why would someone want to throw a ball at somebody else and hit him? Why would anyone want to play a game just to be hit? I don't understand. I've never been with so many boys before. Is this what they think is fun? Why is everyone laughing?

I retreat to the old tree, holding tight to the Devil Dog wrapper. I sit against one of the roots and watch everyone play.

I am different, I realize. I am not like these boys. I am not like any other boy I know.

This feeling did not go away with time. One Saturday morning in September when I was in the sixth grade, my father drove us to a furniture store on the Lynnway to buy a new sofa for our living room. My father liked to think of himself as *avant-garde* when it came to home decor, even though we were hardly the wealthiest in a neighborhood of lower-income families in Lynn. But we were the first to buy a shag carpet that was raked instead of vacuumed. It was our house that boasted a floor poured onto planks of wood then sprinkled with flakes – we got to choose the colors – that within a few hours hardened into the solidified liquid. Problem was, after a few months the floor began to crack, and when my father went to file a complaint, he discovered the company that poured the floor had gone out of business.

That didn't stop him from buying a sofa that none of had ever seen in any of the neighbors' houses. It was deep blue and in three pieces, the middle one curved so it wedged into a corner while the two straight sections lined up against the walls. After the deliverymen carried the sofa into the house in the late afternoon, my father retreated to his den in the basement to spend the rest of the day drinking Knickerbocker beer and smoking Larks. Upstairs, it became clear to my mother that she would no longer be able to sleep on this odd-shaped sofa at night, so she moved her blankets to my sister's bed instead of joining my father in his.

Later that night the *Miss America Pageant* was broadcast from Atlantic City, an evening I had been looking forward to for weeks. I wanted Miss Massachusetts to win as much as most of Boston wanted the Red Sox to clinch the World Series that year. Miss Massachusetts had never captured the crown, but had come in first runner-up when a brunette from Lynnfield performed a sign-language rendition of "What the World Needs Now Is Love Sweet Love" during the talent segment of the evening, which was, along with the evening gown competition, my favorite part of the show.

I tried to get comfortable on the new sofa, but every time I pushed the tiniest bit into the cushions, I could feel the metal springs. I finally settled on my stomach, my chin on the sofa arm. When a parade of women in Catalina swimsuits crossed the screen, it hit me: *I should be feeling something for these women in bathing suits.* Why wasn't I at least as excited about this as I was about the blond ventriloquist from Oklahoma? I slipped my hands into my pajama bottoms to see if I was getting hard. Nothing was happening.

I panicked. I pulled out a medical dictionary that my mother kept in a magazine bin next to the Magnavox TV and her Dean Martin and Jerry Vale albums. The book was hardcover, old, and white; the binding was torn. In the middle of the book was a series of black and white photos. Older women in Aunt Bee dresses clutched purses while they waited in line for a cancer screening. A young boy sat in bed, hair slicked and smiling, his leg in a cast, elevated by a trapeze-like device that hung above him.

I looked up the word *homosexual* in the glossary. I wanted to see who I was; I wanted a mirror, a reflection. I then read that homosexuality was an illness. I was not comforted when I learned that sometimes it could be cured, but only if the patient was willing. The cure involved some sort of shock treatment, electrical currents that would run through my body.

I thought: *Oh, my God. I have it. I'm really sick. This can't be true.*

I slammed the book shut and shoved it back into the bin. I sat in front of the TV again, trying to will myself to be aroused. I would cure myself. I would fix myself before they decided I needed to be zapped with electricity. I didn't sleep that night, imagining my penis connected to an electrical wire in the doctor's office.

On Monday, my father uncharacteristically acknowledged his poor judgment and exchanged the three-piece sofa for a more traditional style. My mother moved her pillow and blanket back into the living room. Everything looked as it did before. But I could never approach the medical dictionary again without worrying that I might have some psychological illness I hadn't heard of, so I only consulted the book to confirm what I thought I already knew: that the cough I had was simply a cold, that the pimple on my chin was acne, and, once, that the lump that had developed behind my knee was a deadly form of cancer, even though weeks later the doctor informed us it was benign.

After elementary school, when hormones started to explode and all my friends were talking about which girls had breasts that had filled out over the summer, my feelings of alienation became public. It started in a locker room, similar to the one at the beach. There were groups of boys to watch as I did on my first day of school, but this time they were older, well into puberty. Girls didn't stir sexual feelings in me, even Miss America contestants, but boys in the school locker room did.

Welcome to gym class.

One of my teachers was a beefy weightlifter who liked to parade around the locker room in skintight shirts and shorts to display his bulging biceps and legs. As he walked, shoulders back, chest out, he used to sing:

I took my girl to the circus
to see what we could see
but when she saw what the elephant had
she wouldn't make out with me.

I pretended to laugh with the rest of the boys, but I hated gym class. I hated the competition, the gang shower requirement, the dank locker room, the fact that I didn't have even a trace of athletic talent. But at least in high school, we weren't required to play basketball every period. Those who were into weight lifting, or simply wanted to avoid the class all together, went to the weight room. Most of the guys did work out, grunting and sweating as their muscles grew bulkier and bulkier. I opted to sit in the corner, occasionally sneaking in a paperback novel that I'd stash away as soon as Mr. Biceps came in to check on us. I'd even mastered the art of shower time: once Biceps checked my name off on his clipboard, I kept the towel wrapped around me and wet my hair quickly under the shower nozzle. He checked my name off once again as I returned to my locker, looking as if I'd showered like the rest of the guys.

Junior high had not been so easy. They kept closer tabs on you in the seventh grade and it was impossible to avoid the shower room.

My troubles started on the very first day of gym class.

All the boys are in the shower room. Mr. Nesson, our tanned gym teacher with sun-bleached hair, controls the water flow from a little booth with an opening that overlooks the room of naked boys. He's the one who, by turning the knob in his booth, ends shower time. He's the one who lets us know when we can leave the room.

It is my first time naked in front of other boys.

I get an erection. I look around and see that it is happening to me and no one else. And everyone else, it seems, finds this repulsive. They nudge each other as they look at me. They stare.

Finally Mr. Nesson, who is still looking from above, turns the water off. I run for a towel, but can't get to one quickly enough before some boys snap me with their towels and push me into the wall.

Faggot.

Queer.

Pussy.

The next few days, before the next gym class, I try to figure out what causes an erection. I decide, without any evidence whatsoever, that not eating or drinking anything the day of the class will prevent further embarrassment.

The day of gym class, I don't eat or drink.

Still, it happens.

That year, every Tuesday and Thursday, I wake up full of dread. I close my eyes in the shower and pray that Mr. Nesson will turn the water off before anyone notices, but he doesn't.

Many years later, when I told my therapist about my gym class, he shook his head.

"There's a word for what happened to you," he said. "Torture."

"Yes, it felt like torture."

"No," he said. "Real torture that you know is coming. Real torture that you know is inevitable. That you can't stop but somebody else can. That gym teacher looking out at you. Did he ever say anything? Do anything?"

"He just watched," I said.

Who knows what was going on outside this old factory town while I was growing up? I didn't. I didn't know about the first gay pride parade in the United States, organized to mark the anniversary of the Stonewall Riots in New York City. I didn't know that the first Hollywood movie to deal openly with homosexuality, *The Boys in the Band*, was playing in movie theaters not far from where I lived. I wasn't aware that the American Psychiatric Association had declared that homosexuality, contrary to what I had read in the medical dictionary, was no long considered an illness. I didn't even know that right in my own back yard, in Massachusetts, Elaine Noble was the first openly gay politician to be elected to state office in the United States.

I only knew of this history long after it became history. The battle for gay marriage was different. By that time I was an openly gay man in a committed relationship. I began to believe that what Heidi Norton and Gina Smith did on March 26th, 2001 – and what six other couples did at their own town halls over the next few days – could be another milestone in a long history that I learned about late, but still in time to keep my sanity. To understand I wasn't alone.

This time I needed to be there.

CHAPTER TWO

REDEFINITIONS

What if instead of opening a medical dictionary to discover who I was, I had opened the newspaper to find out that seven same-sex couples had filed a lawsuit in Suffolk Superior Court in response to their being denied marriage licenses? That rather than considering themselves ill, these couples were so certain that they were nothing more or nothing less than their heterosexual counterparts that they deserved to be treated equally? What if I had read their legal brief online, officially filed on April 11th, 2001, noting that, combined, these couples had shared over 100 years of committed partnership?

I would have read about the normalcy of their lives, how they were parents and grandparents. They were lawyers and business people and teachers and social workers and nurses. They had suffered breast cancer and heart problems. Many had children and had reduced their working hours to spend time with them. Some took care of aging parents, either visiting them frequently or moving them into their homes to provide around-the-clock support. Many were churchgoers, some holding positions of significant responsibility in their congregations. Others were active in their children's schools. They spent holidays with extended families that treated them like married couples. They cared for each other in sickness and in health.

That is, if they were allowed to. The couples told stories of relying on the kindness of strangers to visit each other or their children in the hospital. Even with health care proxies, some had difficulties obtaining medical information about their families. The financial obstacles of caring for each other were even more formidable, and certainly reason enough to marry. But these couples clearly had more in mind when they entered their town halls. Marriage was an emotional, spiritual, and legal commitment as well. In their legal brief, one couple noted that they sought "the emotional peace of mind that comes from being a married couple."

As an adolescent I could never have heard the words "emotional peace of mind" and "gay" in the same breath. I searched for words like these, scouring any book with an index for references under the letter "h." Old habits die hard. I still find myself searching the indices political memoirs or histories. Now I'm at least likely to find a range of opinion, but in the 1960's and 1970's, what I read about myself merely confirmed my suspicions: gay people were ill, to be avoided.

Of course there was an occasional closeted teacher, the one people whispered about, the one everyone loved because he gave everything of himself to his students without ever giving anything away. But mostly gay sexuality was the stuff of scandal. A few years out of high school I heard on the news that one of my male teachers – married to another one of my female teachers – was arrested for having sexual relations with male students. This was not news to those of us who knew him, even if his arrest shocked the community.

There is a profound difference between growing up gay – at least when I was growing up gay – and growing up as a member of a racial minority. Children of color are likely to come home from school to a family that understands and accepts who they are. Gay children in the 60's and 70's – and even now in many places – were likely to live with parents who likely didn't understand and at worst were hostile to homosexuality. My home was no exception.

I grew up surrounded by teeth. Before he owned his convenience store, my father worked as a dental technician in a two-room office on

Monroe Street in downtown Lynn.

One night in the mid-sixties my father received a telephone call: the building was on fire. We piled into the car and raced downtown to see huge flames billowing from the top floor windows. It was immediately clear to us that my father's business as we knew it was over. He'd need to find a new place to run the Northeastern Dental Laboratory.

That new place, my father announced shortly after the fire, would be in our home. He hired a balding Italian man to convert one end of our basement into a workspace. The new Northeastern Dental Laboratory had white paneling and a white-tiled floor. My father managed to salvage some of his more expensive equipment, like the high-temperature oven he used to soften the plastic for dentures. The oven was so hot that the walls inside turned red when it was on. My father tried to scare me into good behavior by turning on the oven, opening the door, and warning me that "hell is hotter than this." He didn't need to say that living well and living a gay life were incompatible. I understood. Hell was the place murderers, rapists, child molesters . . . and gay people went.

My father's laboratory was up and running a few months after the fire. My mother quit her job at a shoe factory to work for him, making his afternoon delivery of dentures to dentists around the North Shore. He wrapped the dentures in tissue paper and put them in manila envelopes. But sometimes he'd take them upstairs for my mother to do the packing, so scattered around the house were false teeth of people I'd never met.

When my father wasn't working in his new office, he was downstairs in the unventilated TV room that smelled of stale beer and cigarette smoke.

I'd watch TV with him on occasion. We rarely talked, except when he'd make a comment during a Red Sox game. One Saturday afternoon we were watching the midday news. A reporter interviewed a man with a beard, who mentioned something about "gay rights."

I'd never heard the word gay before.

"What's *gay* mean?" I asked.

My father sighed, not in exasperation, but in repulsion. He turned and looked directly into my eyes, something he rarely did.

"*Queers*," he said. He clenched his fists, as if to restrain himself.

I'd sit in the sofa while he propped his feet up in the La-Z-Boy chair that I dared use only when he was out doing an errand. When my mother went with him, I'd sometimes play the stereo console, which had long been relegated to a coffee table. It was an unspoken rule that it wasn't to be played anymore; the records would sit there for years, untouched except when I managed to sneak in a few minutes of music.

Sometimes in the basement my father would argue with himself. This usually started about an hour into his nightly intake of six or seven tall cans of beer. He would bite down on his lower lip, then he'd move his jaw, and then he'd start talking, his head bobbing up and down, his eyes squinting. I could rarely make out his words; usually he emitted angry, indecipherable grunts. He could go on like this for hours, his grunts crescendoing now and then, his head jerking.

Years later, I learned a name for this behavior: "shadow boxing." I knew my father was wrestling with demons, but I had never heard this term before. Nor did I ever discover what these shadows in his life were. I only knew they seemed to follow him everywhere, all the time. The very night that he died, a rainy Tuesday in February of 1993, I approached him in the hospital after my mother and sister had left. The room was dark except for the small red and white lights that flashed on one of the machines next to his bed. I walked toward him quietly, trying not to wake him, but as I sat down the stool squeaked, and my father looked up with a start.

"Jesus Christ, Kenny," he blurted. "Why the hell did you have to scare me like that?"

He rolled over, mumbling to himself, boxing his shadows until he died only a few hours later, without ever really knowing who I was.

Who I was and would be. If he had lived, I can't imagine what his reaction would have been to discover that I was one of those *queers* fighting for gay rights. Who knows? Maybe he would have changed his mind when he found out that the plaintiffs who petitioned the court weren't the stereotypes that the media chose to portray all gays and lesbians. Some of the plaintiffs were at least a decade older than he was when he died. And especially for these older couples, the financial obstacles were severe: upon the death of one of the partners, inheritance would be taxed. None of the plaintiffs would collect social security if the other should die. Wills had to be meticulously drawn to ensure that partners received what have been joint property and savings.

Would this have moved my father? Probably not. I'm not even sure he would have understood all the reasons why these couples wanted to marry. What's especially moving about the April 11th brief is not just the usual list of exclusionary practices, but also the focus on the intangible benefits of marriage. What is stated about Heidi Norton and Gina Smith seems to speak for all the couples: they seek "to marry for their own sake, to make a statement about their love and commitment, and . . . they want their two sons to grow up in a world where their parents' relationship is legally and communally respected." Another couple, Gloria Bailey and Linda Davies, wanted "the world to see them as they see themselves – a deeply loyal and devoted couple who are each other's spouses in all ways."

This was not the marriage my parents knew. I never saw my mother and father touch each other – no handholding, no kissing, not even an arm around the shoulder. When my mother's father died and she collapsed in front of the church, my father stood back, and ordered me to help her. Perhaps they had an affectionate life my sister and I never saw. The scenes of their marriage were at times so hard to watch that it wasn't until my sister reminded me of them that I could even begin to piece the fragments of memory together.

"You didn't realize it," she said a few months after our father had died, "but I couldn't stop crying the day you left for college. You were all I had in that family. You were the only sane one."

My sister remembered the insanity better than I did.

"Don't you remember?" she asked me on the phone shortly after my father had died.

"Remember what?"

When I was a child, she told me, I sat on the stairs to our basement and watched my father beat my mother. He dragged her across the shag carpeting and burnt her arm.

She remembers watching me watch the fights, but I don't remember the fights.

My sister would scream at him but I would just sit there, numb, as if I wasn't seeing what I was really seeing.

"You used to throw up a lot," my sister told me. "On the way to school, almost every morning. You'd tell me to wait outside the cemetery gates and then you'd go inside and vomit. Something was really wrong."

I remember the cemetery fence: a mile of pointed black metal poles, one of which, a neighborhood friend told me, pierced the neck of a passenger in a car that had crashed. The passenger lived, the story went, although he still had a piece of metal in his neck.

"You were a mess," my sister told me. "You were picked on at school and tormented at home. I think you made yourself throw up, but I'm not sure. I think you stuck your finger down your throat."

And *I* was the sane one?

I came out to my sister on a Sunday afternoon, on the telephone. She was the first family member I told.

"Ma asked me to ask you if you were gay," she said. "She wants to know if she has a gay son."

Here was my chance. The perfect opening. "Well, she does," I said. I was trembling. If my sister didn't support me, no one in the family would. I waited for a "wow," some expression of surprise.

"You don't think I knew?" she said matter-of-factly. "Of course I knew. I've known since you were a kid."

My sister accepted me immediately; my mother didn't speak to me for years, even though she was the one who asked my sister to pose the question. What she wanted was a denial, even if in her heart she knew. Deception was an unspoken rule in our family.

When I was ten years old or so, my sister was angry. She used to hold her breath until she passed out, and my mother would carry her to the kitchen sink where she would spray cold water on her face. Sometimes she kicked doors; other times she would, as my parents labeled it, become *fresh* or *sassy*. One day my parents had had enough. When I was growing up, she and my father constantly threatened to put me in *reform school* if I misbehaved. They made the place sound worse than Alcatraz. My sister, however, warranted a more severe threat, and they enlisted me in their plan.

I was to come up with the name of a reform school. (I think I eventually came up with something like *The Sunny Day School for Bad Girls*.) I was to type the name of the school on an envelope, address the envelope to my parents, and send it in the mail. When the envelope arrived, they placed it near the telephone, where my sister was sure to see it. No mention was made of the correspondence, but my sister walked around in a depressed daze for weeks.

Even joyous occasions were cloaked in lies. I was informed of my sister's arrival the morning my parents brought her home. She was adopted, yet they convinced me that my mother had given birth to her.

"You're going to get a present this afternoon," my mother said. "What's the one thing you want most in the world?"

I was only five but I knew it was a trick question. Instead of naming what I wanted most, I tried to think of what they thought I wanted most: toy trucks, a GI Joe, a trip to Salem Willows. I never gave the right answer.

"How about a *sister*?" my father finally said.

I remember we were standing in the hallway. Years later, when replaying the scene in my mind, I thought: *Shouldn't we have at least been sitting down?*

"Wow!" I said. I started jumping up and down.

Then the explanation. Did I remember when my mother broke her ankle a few months earlier? How she needed surgery to insert a pin to hold the bones together?

"I had the baby when I was in the hospital with my broken ankle," my mother said to me. "The doctors have been taking care of her all this time."

I believed her, and for the next year or so I thought that anyone who wore a cast was about to give birth. When I started to realize the impossibility of this theory, I confronted my mother as she was ironing.

"The truth is," she said. "Lisa wasn't *expected*; she was *selected*."

Huh? I pictured a row of babies lined up in a maternity ward, my father pointing to my sister as he might select a new car in an automobile sales lot. *Let's give this one a test drive, Edie!*

"Your sister was adopted," my mother clarified. *"Don't ever tell her."*

They never told her. When my sister was about eight or nine years old, we were playing in our neighbor's yard down the street. Out of the blue, one of the girls said to my sister, "You do know you were adopted, don't you?"

My sister looked at me. "That's not true, is it, Kenny?" she asked. I shrugged.

My sister knew.

I don't fully understand why my parents wanted to deny my sister the truth about her birth. They were married in the fifties, a time when the definition of the ideal American family was exceptionally rigid. They used to tell us that my sister and I looked alike, which was ridiculous. We looked nothing alike at all. But maybe my mother's inability to bear children after my birth didn't fit into the family they had imagined for themselves. Maybe the real family they wanted was the one that lived in a white house with a picket fence, the one that owned two cars, a color TV set, and had two heterosexual children who looked just like each other.

Well, we did have the TV set. But by the time I was in high school, my father filed for bankruptcy. We moved from the white house and in with my aunt, who lived in a trailer that she'd transported from the trailer park to a permanent lot. The trailer was expanded on either side in a failed attempt to make it look like a real house. My sister and I used to call it "the truck with wings."

When the addition to the trailer was built, the plans did not include any new walls, so there was little privacy. Only my aunt and my father had real bedrooms with doors. The rest of us slept on sofas and the one other bed that was out in the open, behind the kitchen, original from the trailer. We were in the awkward position of knowing each other's business but were prohibited to discuss our knowledge.

Along with our precarious financial situation, sex was one of those things you never talked about in my family, unless it was some veiled reference that only left me as confused as I was when I associated broken limbs with childbirth. One night my mother sat me down and warned me to "stay away from dirty girls," never considering that I'd eventually take her advice to the extreme and stay away from girls, period. At first I thought that by "dirty" she meant just that: girls with mud on their arms, hair snarled from lack of shampooing, grime under their fingernails. But I later learned that dirty meant diseased. Syphilis and gonorrhea, to be precise. It was the stigma, rather than health concerns, that worried my mother most, as if *The Lynn Daily Evening Item* published lists of the afflicted along with real estate closings for the week. Because my mother never told me exactly how these diseases were contracted, I was convinced I'd been exposed to them on nearly a weekly basis. I didn't know the symptoms, so the deepening of my voice, the appearance of pubic hair, the onset of nocturnal emissions: all that evidence suggested that I was gravely ill.

It wasn't the first time I'd make her uncomfortable with my questions. I don't know where I first heard the words "blow job," but I do remember where I first said the words aloud. In the sixth grade, Wednesday was my day for traffic boy duty, and my mother had to drop me off in front of the school early. We were approaching the crosswalk where I would stand guard when I asked, "What's a blow job?"

"Kenny!" my mother screamed, gripping the steering wheel so as not to lose control but swerving nonetheless. "What did you just say?"

"I asked you what a blow job was."

"Don't you ever say that again."

She pulled to the side of the road.

"I was just wondering," I said, convinced more than ever that I needed to find out what exactly a blow job was.

"I want to know where you heard that word," she demanded, near tears from her anger at me. It was as if I'd committed some egregious sin by not predicting I was about to hear the word so I could block my ears in time.

"I don't know."

"Yes you do, you do to," she said. "Tell me *where*."

"The radio, I guess," I said.

"No you didn't. They don't say things like that on the *radio*."

"I really don't know then."

My mother sighed. "Well, we'll have to put this to rest," she said. "But promise me you won't ever say that word again. You can't even *think* about that word."

"Okay," I said, but of course I knew I could think of little else.

My mother's aversion to sex wasn't based on her religious beliefs. I never knew her to go to church. But she was a member of a group of Catholic women called "Our Lady of Fatima," even though she was raised Protestant. She served as recording secretary of the group which, as far as I could tell, meant that her singular duty was to take minutes for the meetings. While my mother was clearly honored to serve such a role, she was highly anxious about her ability to perform it, and even when I was in junior high, she'd run all her minutes by me for corrections and advice.

"This is important," she would say. "Check it over carefully. Look for spelling and grammar."

My mother was a horrendous speller; it was not unusual for her to write "wuz" instead of "was."

"This is good, Ma," I'd say, not wanting to correct her litany of errors. "This'll be fine."

"No," she said. "I know things are wrong. You've got to tell me. This is important. I don't want to look stupid in front of the girls."

I knew that if I began to correct, most of the words in her minutes would have been crossed out. Despite her pleas for me to tell her what was wrong, I was sure she would take so many corrections with great offense. She often told me that my father gave her "a complex," a term I didn't completely understand but sensed it meant she was lacking in confidence.

"Why don't I just type the minutes for you?" I asked her. "I want to practice typing. Why don't I just type them for you and I'll make the corrections as I go along?"

"Okay," she said. "That would be good. Just give me them to me after you're done."

I corrected all the errors and gave the typed sheets to her.

"Look at this," she said. "You need to *write out* the number 5. Don't just put the number. These are the *records* of the group. Don't you understand? You're going to have to type the whole thing over."

When I was thirty-seven I typed for my mother a final time: I wrote her a letter telling her I was gay. I edited it almost as many times as I'd edit one of my short stories, then dropped it in a mailbox.

My mother called me as soon as she opened the letter. She was crying. How could I upset her so? Why had I done this? She needed to talk to me.

"We need to clear the air," she said.

We cleared the air in a dirty compact car in the parking lot of the Burlington Mall. My mother leaned against the driver's door, folding her arms and looking directly at me.

"Why did you do this?" she asked.

"It wasn't something I *did*," I said. "It's something I *am*."

"And you choose *now* to tell me?"

"Why not now?"

"Now that you father's dead?"

I knew he wouldn't have been much support to her if he had been alive. I could even imagine him telling her that it was her fault I was gay. *You made a sissy of him. You let him quit his paper route. You let him buy figure skates instead of hockey skates.*

"I thought that you'd want to know this about me," I said. "I didn't want to keep it a secret any longer."

"I wish I was with your father right now," she said. "I wish I was *dead*."

I gulped. I had heard her suicide threats since I was a child. When I was a young boy she would tell me how she had taken too many pills and had too many glasses of Wild Irish Rose wine. "I was laying on the dining room floor," she'd say. "I wanted God to take me. I wanted to leave this world."

"You can't do this to me," I said in the car. "You've been doing this to me since I was a kid. You can't do this anymore."

My uncharacteristic directness seemed to temporarily silence her. She stared at me for a moment, puzzled, then continued with more questions. *What about AIDS? What will people think? What about your job? And* the final questions, her greatest concern: *What about me? What will happen to me now? Did you ever think of that?*

So that was it. She needed to be cared for, something she never experienced in her marriage. I tried to get her to open up.

"Look, I know being married to dad wasn't easy. I feel for you."

Her eyes widened incredulously. "How *dare* you say that about your father!"

I said nothing else except good-bye. I shut the door and walked to my car. My mother pulled out of the parking space, floored the car, then screeched the brakes as she stopped in front of me. She rolled down her window.

"Just remember I love you," she screamed, then floored the car again.

It was love as a drive-by shooting.

When I first read the complaint filed by the gay couples who were denied marriage licenses, I was struck by some words one usually doesn't associate with a legal brief: love, support, joy, commitment. The plaintiffs – carefully chosen by GLAD (Gay and Lesbian Advocates and Defenders) and Mary Bonauto, its attorney – redefined not just everything I had learned about gay people growing up. It also redefined a great deal of what I learned about families.

CHAPTER THREE

RELIGIOUS EDUCATION

If I had read about the plaintiff couples when I was a teenager, much about their lives would have surprised me – their families' acceptance, their children, the deeply felt love and commitment – but nothing would have been more foreign to me than learning that four of the eight couples were affiliated with churches. Being gay and having a religion were simply incompatible when I was growing up.

I was raised a Roman Catholic. When I was in first or second grade, my father gave me a book on Catholicism written for children. I don't remember much about what the book said, but one page made an indelible impression on me. It was a drawing of hell, complete with flames, devils, burning bodies and pitchforks. It remains so clear in my mind that over forty years after seeing it, I could recreate the image on canvas if I'd been born with even a modicum of artistic talent.

In the drawing, there are four devils, all with horns and holding pitchforks, all shirtless and goateed. One is standing in the forefront, his muscular torso facing us, his pitchfork stabbing into a burning, naked body whose back is to us so as not to expose the genitals. Flames cover the buttocks. There are other naked bodies, all tactfully covered with fire, all male, but this particular man's body is the one I remember. And the man's face: his eyes rolled up, his jaw dropped, his head flung back in resigned anguish.

I returned to the drawing again and again, only to close the book tight, petrified of my possible fate after death. When I wasn't looking at the drawing, I thought of it. I dreamed of it. I didn't consider its homoeroticism until years later when I realized that the expression on the naked body was more ecstatic than anguished. The message was at once subtle and clear: homoerotic attraction and perpetual pain went hand in hand.

This wasn't the only time I would hear the Catholic Church say "come hither" only to realize I would be damned for eternity if I accepted the invitation. When I was in high school, I visited all the Catholic churches in Lynn and the surrounding cities the evening before Good Friday. At each church I'd pray at the Stations of the Cross: sometimes they were stained glass windows, sometimes they were relief sculptures. What I remember most about these images was Jesus in his loincloth, which was as low as it could be without revealing his genitals. In these images his body was firm and toned, even though blood dripped from his palms. I knew I shouldn't be thinking about him in this way but I did, convinced I would join the burning bodies in the book if I didn't stop.

In college I majored in Spanish and studied a great deal of Golden Age literature. When I first read the poetry of the Spanish mystics, I was seduced by the homoeroticism of the church once more. These mystics told me that the meeting with God in the afterlife was a *sexual* union. As a child, I certainly had never envisioned what St. John of the Cross described in his poetry, which was filled with the most homoerotic yearning I'd ever read. In his union with God, St. John plays with his "beloved's" hair. He caresses him while he sleeps. He asks that his lover "now consummate" and pleads with him to "tear through the veil of this sweet encounter."

How else could a gay man interpret these poems? And how else could a gay man not be confused? If I happened to take these words at face value, if I happened to feel the erotic energy that pulsated these lines, I was told that I would end up in flames. The image of the horned devil, roasting me, using his pitchfork to turn my body over as if to make sure I was evenly cooked, was there. It was there, no matter how much I could laugh when I realized its absurdity and manipulation.

And so I prayed to be different, to not feel these feelings the church was at once asking me to feel then warning of punishment if I did.

I prayed and prayed and prayed.

I finally left the Catholic Church after I graduated from college, but its influence was never far from reach. As the battle for same-sex marriage heated up in Massachusetts, I found myself confronting my Catholic upbringing perhaps more than any other time in my adult life. Many organizations opposed same-sex marriage, but none did so more vocally and passionately than the church where I spent my childhood and young adulthood.

By the time the Court of Appeals ruled against the eight plaintiffs – over two years after the couples had filed their complaint – and, almost a year after that, the Massachusetts Supreme Judicial Court (SJC) began hearing the plaintiffs' appeal, the Catholic Church was awash in scandal. Only three months before the SJC began their deliberations, Catholic Archbishop Cardinal Bernard Law resigned in disgrace at the height of what the Attorney General Tom Reilly called the "the greatest tragedy to befall children – ever" in Massachusetts: the clergy sexual abuse scandal. Reilly accused church leaders of "sacrificing children for many years" and said, "The mistreatment of children was so massive and so prolonged that it borders on the unbelievable." Some 237 priests were accused of sexually molesting at least 789 minors. The evidence is overwhelming that church leaders knew the extent of the crisis, yet in the six decades leading up to Cardinal Law's resignation, the church alerted law enforcement authorities of its knowledge of sexual abuse by its priests only twice.

It was against this backdrop that the Boston Archdiocese responded to the possibility that gay men and lesbians could marry. Cardinal Sean O'Malley, who had replaced Law after his resignation, was unwavering in his opposition not only to gay marriage, but also limited domestic partner benefits, calling such arrangements "an attack on the public good." And while it was mere coincidence that the issue of gay marriage and the revelations of clergy sex abuse scandal took place more or less simultaneously, the leaders of the Catholic Church made certain that the two events were linked. Even though priests had abused both boys and girls, the church's attention was almost exclusively on the abuse of young boys. O'Malley went so far as to state that allowing gay marriage would exacerbate the problem of child abuse in the United States. The message was clear: gay men and lesbians could not be trusted with children.

The Vatican responded to the sexual abuse tragedy not by reflecting on its own role in the cover up, but by asking seminaries to consider whether or not gay men should be allowed into the priesthood. Said Vatican spokesman Dr. Joaquin Navarro-Valls, "People with these inclinations just cannot be ordained," echoing what had been written earlier by former Vatican official Cardinal Jorge Arturo Medina Estevez: "a homosexual person . . . is not suitable to receive the sacrament of holy orders." Shortly after Mary Bonauto presented arguments for the seven gay couples to the Massachusetts SJC, the Catholic newspaper *The Pilot* quoted psychiatrist Richard Fitzgibbons in an editorial: "The majority of persons experiencing same-sex attraction have histories" including "childhood traumas, developmental deficits, and/or relationship problems."

These stereotypes of gay men as mentally ill pedophiles were an eerie *deja vu* for me. I had spent years trying to erase these visions of gay men that everyone, as the lyrics of the song about racism in *South Pacific* says, "carefully taught" me. And one of the teachers was, not surprisingly, the Catholic Church. Certainly I remember the lessons I learned in books – the picture of the naked burning men is the most vivid – but I also learned through experience.

As president of the Catholic Youth Organization (CYO) at our church, I once found myself at a meeting with Father McCarthy, the CYO adult advisors, and my fellow officers. The issue was dancing. *Slow* dancing. *The bear hug*, as Father McCarthy called it. This type of dancing was immoral, he said. It needed to stop at CYO dances or he would have to shut them down.

"I don't get it," I said at meeting to discuss the issue. "I don't understand what the sin is here. Nothing's happening, right? It's not like people are making out."

That's when Father McCarthy delivered his impromptu sermon on the *near occasion of sin*. This was when we put ourselves in a position when sin is likely. We're almost there, but not quite. I looked up the term on the Internet many years later and found a web site with the heading, "How to Avoid the Near Occasion of Sin." Apparently, simply being on the Internet was considered "the near occasion," because it was suggested that a picture of the Blessed Mother be taped to the computer so that you could look at her while surfing the net. Her very image would keep you in line.

I didn't think much about the near occasion of sin until a year or so later. As CYO president, I was in the parish rectory often, conferring with all the priests and, especially, the new advisor to our group, Father Leland. We all loved Father Leland. He was funny and young and listened to rock music. He wasn't stuffy like Father McCarthy.

One Sunday evening, I visited the rectory with a friend. I don't remember exactly why; we probably had to get Father Leland's okay for an activity we were planning. He greeted me with his warm smile and laughter that cut through the oppressive silence of the building. My friend sat down in the living room to talk with Father McCarthy while Father Leland asked me into his room. Would I like to hear some Pink Floyd? I immediately said I would. Wow. How could he be a priest and like Pink Floyd? I browsed through his stack of records. The Who. Yes. The Rolling Stones. This was the coolest priest I'd ever met.

I sat cross-legged on the floor as father Leland put on the LP, and we listened for a few minutes through the occasional snaps and crackles of the record. Then, seemingly out of nowhere, Father Leland began talking about loneliness. He talked about the role of masturbation in lonely men's lives.

I wasn't sure I'd heard him right. No one had ever talked to me about masturbation before. I wasn't scared, just bewildered. In the early seventies no one talked about priests as being sexually inappropriate. I didn't know enough to be concerned. But I was confused. I didn't know what Father Leland wanted from me. Was this a door to talk about my own masturbatory life? Did he think I was lonely, even though I was hardly "a man"? Was he the lonely man who masturbated? I didn't know what to say.

He then told me it was normal to masturbate at my age. I became flustered, embarrassed. Although the room was dimly lit, I wondered if he could see me turning red. He had a book on the topic, he said.

My friend came in from his conversation in the living room, and our conversation ended. I kept my distance from Father Leland from then on. I don't know if I worried that he might go beyond simply discussing about masturbation, but I was certain I didn't want to talk about it. It wasn't until many years later, after news of the sex abuse scandal broke, that I saw my stepping back from him as an act of self-preservation.

It's quite possible that by questioning his intentions, I'm doing Father Leland a grave injustice. Maybe he had nothing inappropriate in mind.

Or maybe this was the real near occasion of sin.

I learned something else from the Catholic Church: God was a sadistic Peeping Tom. He was like Santa Claus – he knew when I was sleeping, awake, bad or good – but unlike Santa didn't stop at a few lumps of coal in a stocking to make his point.

And when God was busy, Sister Alexandrine, my Sunday school teacher in fifth grade, took his place.

She must have been in her seventies. Her bandeau and coif looked like white cardboard so tightly fitting that her cheeks puffed out. Chains and ropes draped from her waist. A large, heavy crucifix hung from her neck, resting right below the large white panel that covered her breasts, like a bib. I sometimes wondered if she'd have worn an electric chair if Jesus had been killed in the twentieth century.

Sister Alexandrine had a glass eye. I'd never known anyone with a glass eye before. A friend of my father's had a sleepy eye; it would drift off to the side so that his two pupils never aligned. But a glass eye was completely different. It seemed just a little too big for Sister Alexandrine's face. I don't remember the color, but I do remember that the color didn't seem *real*, that it didn't match her other eye. It didn't move at all, and seemed to be staring at something invisible to the rest of us.

But the weirdest thing of all was that Sister Alexandrine could *see* out of that eye. I swear. It was the Eye of God.

I know this to be true because I sat on the left side of the room, in the row closest to the wall, and it was her right eye that was made of glass. Yet she saw everything I did: passing notes, making faces at my friends, doodling when I should have been writing, dozing off. She noticed my transgressions immediately, armed with her litany of punishments that included standing in a wastepaper basket in front of the room, being sent to the girls' classroom for the rest of the morning, or splaying our fingers on the desks so she could whack them with the dreaded metal ruler.

But that eye: it became a symbol for me of the all-knowing God, the God that not only saw what I was *doing*, but could see right into my brain and know what I was *thinking*. And this power to read my mind throughout much of my childhood that petrified me.

I tried to trick the Glass Eye by tacking photos of Cybill Shephard and Ali MacGraw on my bedroom walls. I thought that just maybe I might able to get away with it. Just maybe the Glass Eye might have one too many minds to read and would only give me a perfunctory going-over: the outwards signs of my heterosexuality would be enough.

But this was not a permanent solution. I knew that the real answer was in somehow altering my mind. I tried telling myself over and over not to think of men, which of course immediately filled my mind with images of them. So I designed a new strategy. Whenever I thought of men I would pinch myself as hard as I could. Maybe after time my brain would listen, and I would be normal.

All I got were deep red pinch marks. Nothing changed. And Sister Alexandrine's eye – *God's* eye – kept watching me, night and day, keeping score of my impure thoughts.

I went through most of the late seventies and eighties believing I was not worthy of a spiritual life. If I wasn't out of the closet, I was certainly becoming more and more aware of who I was sexually. But much of the time I was able to slip into a convenient state of denial, where I could consider my sexuality far more ambiguous than it really was. I had sex with women and convinced myself I enjoyed it, which I suppose I did at some level. But what was missing was any sense of passion, of eroticism, of desire. It was pleasurable enough, in a rather "why not?" sort of way. But this was what I was supposed to be doing. This was what my father expected, who shortly after I graduated from college, asked me when I was going to bring some girl home and start to settle down. He hadn't seen a girl I'd dated since my high school girlfriend, a relationship that was far more comforting than it was sexual since she seemed to have as little interest in getting laid as I did.

And then there was the expectation of the church. When I was living in Madrid after college, I met a Spaniard who was a member of the Catholic group *Opus Dei*, a group I had never heard of but have since learned about. We'd meet occasionally at his apartment and sing while he clumsily played the guitar: The Beatles and The Mamas and The Papas and Loggins and Messina. Shortly after we met he told me he was praying for me; he wanted me to get married and have children. "You'll be a wonderful father," he told me. Even though I considered being a wonderful father a supreme compliment, I was furious but said nothing, for fear he'd question the source of my anger. What right did this person I barely knew have to pray for me? To tell me what my lot in life should be? And there was no denying the anxiety in his voice when he talked about his prayers for me. He knew who I was, I am certain of this in hindsight, and wanted to save me.

If I hadn't already stopped going to Mass, this might have been the moment I threw up my hands and left the Catholic Church. I was angry, yes. But my conversation with my Spanish friend was also the moment I was convinced no church would have me and that I would have no church. I've since come to believe that one of the most egregious myths many gay kids grow up believing is that they can have no spiritual home.

I was wrong, of course. In my thirties, I did find a spiritual home. And as impossible as it seemed to me when I was in my teens and twenties, I married a man – both legally and spiritually – in a church.

CHAPTER FOUR

VISIBILITY

By the summer of 2003, the *Goodridge* case had gone before the Massachusetts SJC and its decision was expected any day. Bruce and I were taking our vacation in Stratford, Ontario, where we had been attending the theater festival there since we met. SJC decisions are frequently released on Tuesdays, so while we were in Stratford we went to the local library to check the Internet for news. We didn't check only on that Tuesday, but every other day as well on the slim chance that the court opted not to announce its ruling on the traditional day.

I was so engaged in the *Goodridge* case that the announcement of another court decision – perhaps even more important than *Goodridge* – took me by surprise. This United States Supreme Court case was *Lawrence v. Texas*, and some scholars believe that it is to gay people what *Brown v. Board of Education* was to African-Americans. In a sweeping 6-3 ruling that surprised even the most optimistic observers, the court declared that the sodomy laws in a number of states were unconstitutional. In the 1980's the court had upheld such laws, so the *Lawrence* decision wasn't just a ruling; it was also an overruling.

Bruce worked a good deal in Texas at the time, often referring to his business trips as periods when he was an "unconvicted felon." While his tone was joking, he was speaking the truth: the very fact of our relationship made us criminals in some states. The two of us, like Tyrone Garner and John Geddes Lawrence, the two men who were arrested for having sexual relations in the *Lawrence* case, could have been arrested. And like Garner and Lawrence, we could have been arrested not for any public sexual activity, but activity in the privacy of our own bedroom. Of course, it's hard to imagine a scenario where the police would witness private, consensual sexual activity, but that was exactly the scenario when police barged into John Geddes Lawrence's apartment on a phony drug charge. They were immediately arrested for breaking the Homosexual Conduct Law, which prohibited anal and oral sex by two people of the same gender, but not by heterosexual couples.

While the Massachusetts couples were prepared for the onslaught of press coverage, Lawrence and Garner were quiet, publicity-shy men who had so little experience in public speaking that their lawyers had to shield them from the media. They may not have been handpicked to be the faces of a movement, but with their photographs now on the front page of *The New York Times*, they had lost the comfort of their anonymity. They had come out to the entire country, exchanging their privacy for visibility.

The word "privacy" is such a double-edged sword for gay people. I believe, as I think most gay people believe, that our relationships should be protected because they *are* private and consensual. At the same time, the word is also used to condemn same-sex couples that dare even hold hands in public. For us it's called a private matter, unlike when heterosexual couples engage in any public display of affection. Most of my life I've heard supposedly open-minded people say that they have nothing against gay people as long as they don't "flaunt" their sexuality. The bar for flaunting is very low: sometimes a mere arm around the shoulders will do it.

In essence, Lawrence and Garner were forced out of the closet on a national – even international-scale. They didn't ask for the attention. The alternative was to plead guilty to the charge against their sexual relationship. But they asked the question every gay person asks him or herself: how visible do I want to be? Sometimes the answer is easy. The stakes are too high *not* to be visible. Or the reverse: yes, there are still parts of the country where the risk is too high *to* be visible. But for many if us, at least for my generation, deciding whether or not to be visible – or deciding *how* visible to be – is a soul-searching decision.

I've been visible as a gay man for almost twenty years now. That is, it's been that long since I've chosen to be visible. There have been other times when my visibility has affected the way people perceived me. I've had no moments nearly as significant as the Lawrences and Garners and Goodridges of the world, of course, but I dare say most of us don't really want those moments. I'm happy enough when a straight eighth grade boy comes to me, which he did shortly after I came out to my students, wanting to talk about problems he was having with his girlfriend. I was stunned; one of the things I feared most about coming out to kids was the negative effect it might have on heterosexual boys. Would they now feel uncomfortable with me? Not this boy, at least. "Thanks Mr. Harvey," he said after we spoke. "You just seemed like the type of person I could talk to about these things."

Above all, I've learned, kids value authenticity in adults.

There have been other times when I was visible even though I didn't want to be, times when I didn't want to be visible even to myself. I wanted to slip on the comfortable shoes of denial, even if those shoes eventually wear out at the sole, exposing your bare feet to glass and sharp rocks and burning hot pavement.

I spent the year after college traveling throughout Spain on a Thomas J. Watson grant to study the changes in the theater since Franco's death. I had been in Madrid since August, and I'd decided to spend a few weeks in April away from the city, which was cold and drizzly. I rented a room in Málaga for a week and took the bus to Torremolinos for the day trip. I had read about the town in *The Drifters*, the James Michener novel we'd all devoured in high school. We came of age in the seventies, the decade of ambivalence and apathy, and we desperately wanted to identify with a different era. *The Drifters* took place in the sixties, and it defined who many of us wanted to be.

I was lonely in Spain. I'd made a few friends in Madrid, had dated a couple of women there, and convinced myself I was heartbroken when we split up. But for the most part I was a solo traveler. Except for a quick flight from Boston to Washington, DC, when I was a senior in college, I'd never even been on a plane before arriving in Madrid. I was now living in a country where, although I knew the language, I hardly knew a soul.

I was also feeling unsettled, not just because of my lack of connection in Spain, but because a series of world events. Within a few months, Ronald Reagan had been shot, the Pope had been shot, and John Lennon had been killed. Most frightening was the coup attempt in Spain: a handful of national police stormed the Spanish Parliament, armed with machine guns, and tried to take over the government. That night, the few people I knew were packing their bags to flee to Portugal, fearful that their left-leaning politics would put them in danger with a new dictatorship. The coup had failed by the next morning, but I couldn't shake the uneasiness of that night for the rest of my time in Spain. So I did what I often did when I became anxious: I traveled.

I took a dislike of Torremolinos before I'd even gotten off the bus. Missing was the old Spanish charm I'd so loved about Madrid. Instead of quaint *pensiones,* all I could see through the bus window were generic slabs of hotels that blocked the Mediterranean Sea from the inland. Tourists roamed the streets in a daze from boredom and hangovers. I'd arrived expecting the sixties, and got the seventies, with some sixties drugs added in for good measure. Now I had seven or eight hours here. I considered checking the schedule for the next bus back to Málaga, but I decided to give the town at least an hour, so I headed toward the beach where I removed my topsiders and walked. It was sunny, and I soaked in the warmth, hoping it might lift my spirits. I looked for a spot against the wall where I could sit and read the Agatha Christie novel I had bought at an English bookstore in Madrid before leaving for the south. Reading my own language for a change was comforting, like watching a favorite movie again. I dug my toes into the white sand.

"*José?*" A tall blond man – late twenties, early thirties, I guessed – cocked his head with a smile of recognition.

"No," I said in Spanish. "I'm afraid you mistaken me for someone else."

"You look *just like him*," he said. "It's amazing." He looked at the book I was carrying. "Ah! Are you are from England?"

I told him that I spoke English but that I was American. The conversation shifted to English, even though his wasn't very good.

He told me his name was Stefan. I was relieved to be talking to anyone since I'd spent so many of my days hardly saying a word. He was a journalist, he said, vacationing from Germany. His parents owned an apartment that overlooked the ocean, and they had given it to him for a few weeks. Would I like to see it? It was within walking distance.

I immediately said yes. *This* was how my entire year was supposed to be: meeting strangers who immediately wanted to connect. This is what I'd heard about from so many college friends who had "done" Europe. You meet people, they told me. They introduce you to other people. Trust me, they said. You'll have friends in no time. Yet I could name only two so far, both at the pension where I stayed in Madrid: Antonio, a telephone worker from the Canary Islands who wanted me to teach him English, and Ana, a deeply depressed woman from northern Spain who was addicted to drugs and constantly complained that her bones hurt.

"I am thinking of having the party this evening," Stefan said. "I would like it very much for you to attend."

"That would be great," I said. I envisioned an address book filled with new friends I would meet. Suddenly I loved Torremolinos.

Stefan escorted me into the dark lobby of a building my parents would have called "ritzy." We took the elevator to his apartment, which was near the very top. He showed me the balcony. It overlooked miles and miles of ocean.

"This is beautiful," I said.

"I spend all the day out here," he said. "Just to read and to the listening to radio. It is not necessary for you to wear the clothes. No one sees."

I smiled but only removed my shirt.

Stefan shrugged. He disrobed and stood naked in front of me. I began doubting myself: *hey, you wanted sixties, you got sixties. Nude sun-*

bathing. He'll probably offer you a joint in a few minutes. Don't be so uptight. Just relax, pretend this is no big deal.

So I opened my book and read. I tried to focus on the words, but this became impossible once I realized that Stefan had an erection and was masturbating, making me his audience. I was struck with paralyzing dread. I don't think I was afraid that Stefan would force me to have sex, although here, too, I might be revealing more than a little naiveté. The danger seemed more emotional than physical or sexual. I was petrified that he'd recognized in me what I'd tried to bury even from myself. Why did he assume after such a brief exchange on the beach that I might be interested in having sex with him? Or even just watching him have sex with himself? I found myself alternately looking away from him and hating myself as I stole a glance, only to look away when he saw me watching him.

"It is okay," he said. "You only should relax."

I looked away. I looked at him. I looked away again.

He said nothing else. His breathing hardly changed, which only made the situation feel more dangerous. Had he done this with so many young men that it had completely lost its erotic charge? As soon as he came, he reached over to a small table next to my chair and pulled a tissue from a box to clean himself, as if the box had been placed there for that very purpose.

"I have to go," I said suddenly, gathering my sneakers and backpack. "I've forgotten something I was supposed to do."

Stefan looked bemused; he could see right through my lie, of course.

"Are you certain you do not want to remain here?"

"No, really. It's time for me to leave." I didn't even bother to put on my sneakers before I headed to the door. As I ran to the elevator, I heard Stefan yell "Good-bye," then stop as if he'd forgotten my name. It was then that I realized that the entire *you look just like José* line had been a setup that had worked for Stefan over and over again.

As I passed the reception desk, I slowed down to give a casual, "Buenos días" to the elderly clerk. I didn't want to appear too anxious in front of him; then *he* might be able to see right through me like Stefan.

I started running again when I reached the street. The pavement burned the balls of my feet. I didn't stop until I found my way to the bus stop and bought an early ticket back to Málaga. I found a single seat near the back of the bus, where I finally calmed down.

I put on my sneakers again.

Here I was safe from Stefan. Here I was safe from myself.

When I returned from Spain, I began working at a private boarding school where I taught Spanish, advised the yearbook staff, and, perhaps most demanding of all, helped run a dormitory of forty or so high school boys. My apartment was two cement cubicles joined by a tiny bathroom. A toaster oven on the floor served as my kitchen; a legless, torn armchair served as my living room.

Keeping any semblance of order during the evening study hall period in the dormitory was a major challenge. One particularly unruly night, I tried everything to keep the noise down. I cajoled. I promised rewards of extra TV time later in the evening. Then, against my instincts, I became inflexible. *No, you can't walk down the hall to get your homework from Andrew. No, you can't listen to your stereo while you work. No, it doesn't matter if you wear headphones. No. No. No.*

It was during one of my more uncompromising moments that I pissed off Robert, a muscular, blond senior who was years ahead of me in physical maturity with his perpetually stubbled chin. I was two years out of college and I couldn't even grow a mustache. If our school had a football team, Robert would have been a shoe-in. As it was, he was a star soccer player and wrestler.

I told Robert it was time to study.

"I need to talk to Greg," he said.

"Sorry Robert," I said. "Settle down first; then we'll talk about seeing Greg."

"But I have a math test."

"Robert, please. It's time to."

"I'll flunk because of you."

"Not now, Robert."

"Fuck you, you faggot. I'll kill you."

He slammed down his books and retreated to the bathroom. I stood in the doorway, waiting for an apology, but he didn't return.

I was not out to anyone, but the word *faggot* resonated deeper than the threat. He knew about me, even though I thought I was invisible. I walked down to my supervisor's apartment and knocked on his door. I explained what had just happened.

"He called me a faggot," I said before I told him about the threat. "Nobody calls me a faggot." My response was ambiguous, even to me: did the word offend me because I was, in fact, gay? Or was I offended at being seen as gay?

My supervisor, Robert's coach, had a talk with him. Robert got a work detail. He had to dust the shelves of the library for an hour.

Word spread among the boys. *Robert called Harvey a faggot.* The label stuck, although it was rarely said to my face again. But a few boys saw my new status as resident closeted homosexual as a sign of weakness, as a license to ignore any authority I had whatsoever. Once, when I asked a senior who towered over me to get to study hall, he continued to joke with his friends. Finally I said, "Come, on. Just get to your room and study. Don't be an ass." This was the tenor of dorm life, a casualness that marked the relationships between the men and the boys. I'd heard men say far worse in their joking.

But I was not these other men.

The senior grabbed me by the collar and slammed me against the brick wall of the dormitory hallway.

"You don't ever call me an ass again," he said. "You say that again and I'll take you down so fast you won't know what hit you."

I should have known I couldn't deal with kids the way my straight colleagues in the dorm did.

I never told anyone what had happened. I was afraid. Afraid the rumors about me would intensify. Afraid my colleagues would find out about me. Afraid that I would become even more visible than I already was. Afraid that he really would take me down.

To stop the rumors and to try to assure myself they weren't true, I started dating another teacher at the school, a woman who had the reputation of being incapable of settling down, which, of course, was of great comfort to me. In bed one night she told me she had been with many women in her life, an acknowledgment that comforted me even more. The she said, "I'm just assuming you've been with men. You're bisexual too, aren't you?"

"Not really," I said. "But it's completely fine with me if you sleep with women." I sounded sickeningly noble, when in fact I was thinking, *now I don't have to feel guilty if I can't really love you the way I'm supposed to.* I suppose the relationship was what we now refer to as "friends with benefits," but these were benefits I could never really take advantage of, a little like tuition reimbursement for children of faculty at the school when I had no children.

I was miserable in the relationship and so was she. When we broke up, she started dating women again, while I retreated to my teaching, spending more hours than necessary preparing for classes, reading student work two or three times, joining any committee that would welcome me.

I was beginning to learn how profound the silence of the closet really was. It not only shut your lips; it tied your hands. It rendered you helpless.

I first began thinking seriously that I might come out – actually speak aloud the words that described who I was to someone else – shortly after my father died. He'd been sick with bladder cancer for almost two years. Just as he denied so much in his life – his violence, his alcoholism – so too did he deny his own illness. It wasn't until my mother, cleaning the bathroom in the remodeled trailer they were living in at the time, saw that my father had forgotten to flush the toilet and the bowl was filled with bloody urine. When she confronted him, he said the bleeding had been going on for quite some time, but he was convinced that he had strained himself taking out the trash one evening.

His death was in some ways a relief. No matter how strained our relationship, it was painful to see him suffer. I was moved to tears the night I met him in the emergency ward where he sat, a baseball cap over his bald head and a blanket around his shoulders like the cape of some cartoon hero. He'd had what they called a chemo burn, which had left him weak and alternately cold and feverish.

His imminent death made it less frightening for me to finally come to grips with being gay. I didn't talk much about him to Dr. Frum, a sixty-something heavyset psychiatrist who picked the lint off her plaid flannel skirt as I spoke. I talked about wanting to meet someone, and when she assumed I meant a woman, I played along. She gave me astute dating tips like "people usually have sex after the third date" and "think ahead about what you're going to say before asking a woman out." Once, as a snowstorm whirled outside during our session, she looked out the window while I was speaking and said, "I don't know how I'll ever make it home."

My insurance covered eight weeks, after which I stopped going, despite a note from Frum urging me to return to say good-bye. I didn't return to therapy until a year after my father died. I called another therapist who agreed to see me the following week. When he asked me about my sexual orientation I said, "I'm straight. Maybe there's a little bisexuality in there, but I'm basically straight."

He asked me some other questions about my life. He asked me about sleep patterns and dreams.

I hadn't planned on telling him as much as I did. I thought I might talk to him a little at a time. I thought that maybe, if I trusted him, in a few weeks I might say I was questioning my sexual orientation. Wasn't that why I'd called him in the first place?

Maybe. Maybe not. I suddenly had no idea why the fuck I was in the office.

I started telling him of my recurring nightmares. My fear of being touched. I told him about the shreds of memory that would come and go. There were images, real if incomplete, that haunted me. An adult coming into bed with me in the middle of the night when I was nine or ten on an overnight trip away from home. Someone trying to wrestle me out of my bathing suit. Standing naked in front of some staring people, a preadolescent on the verge of growing public hair while a boy kept pointing at my penis and asking me what it was.

I don't see faces, I told my therapist. I remember the physical world around me: the chenille bedspread over my head as I was touched, the warm ground on my bare feet as I was urged to disrobe, the cold linoleum floor where I stood on exhibition. Why can't I remember anything else? I asked.

He explained to me that denial can be a good thing, that our minds remember what we're ready to remember, and that someday, if my mind and body were strong enough, I might remember more; but I needed to accept that the picture might always be lacking. I came to see these pieces of memory like the debris after an airplane crash. I might never see the actual explosion, but I could see the smoking wreckage. That was enough. We could work with that.

But my sister remembers, I told my new therapist that first session. She remembers how I would throw up every time I'd go to the house with the chenille bedspread. She knows some things I never have been able to remember.

"I think you have post traumatic stress disorder," my therapist said.

"What's that?" I asked.

He explained what it was. People who have gone through some sort of trauma carry that trauma with them. We see extreme cases after soldiers return from war or when children witness atrocities. He talked about meds, about seeing him once a week.

"Okay," I said.

"You are depressed, too," he said. "We'll need to deal with that."

"Okay," I said, and then I added, "I think I'm gay."

"Are you attracted to men?" he asked.

"Yes," I said. "Yes, I am."

Of course, coming out to one person – and a professional, at that – was only the beginning. I gradually told friends and acquaintances. That seemed enough to me. I had no intention of telling colleagues, and certainly not students. That changed in October, 1994.

I was in bed, alone. I lay in the dark. My mind wandered to my to-do list for the next day, what I didn't get done on my to-do list today, my writing, how much I loved autumn, how uncomfortable my futon mattress is, and then, as is often true when I have time to think, my past.

I thought about how ashamed I was that I didn't come out earlier than I did. That I waited until I was thirty-four years old.

I thought about how lucky I was that I didn't come out in my early twenties, right when AIDS was being spread, unbeknownst to the gay men who were having sex. I thought about how I used AIDS to keep myself from having sex in my late twenties and early thirties. Why take the chance? I told myself, when, of course, it was the emotional chance, not the physical one, that most scared me.

I thought about the men I knew who had already died. I didn't know as many as most gay men did, but I knew enough. I thought about how I could have been one of them.

I was ashamed and I was lucky.

I thought about the suicides, the attempted suicides, of kids I knew, of friends I knew.

I thought about David, the gay man I knew in graduate school who never mentioned the deep scar across his wrist that I noticed one morning at breakfast.

I thoight about Gregory, an advisee of mine when I taught high school, who was sleeping with his roommate and who, a few years after graduation, put a gun to his head and killed himself.

I thought about Jacob, a gay student I proctored in college, who jumped to his death off the Golden Gate Bridge .

I thought about Robert, another gay man I knew from college, who also jumped to his death, in full drag, out a window.

I thought about Shawn Hughes.

I'd been thinking about Shawn Hughes a lot. About a week earlier, I had been in my apartment reading *Bay Windows*, the gay newspaper in Boston. On the front page was a piece by a young man who talked about growing up gay. Three attempted suicides. Bouts of depression that sent him to the hospital. "If I had only had an out gay teacher to talk to," he wrote, "my life would have been completely different."

I realized the author was Shawn Hughes, the same Shawn Hughes I taught in the eighties. With his red-dyed hair and multiply pierced ears, he had earned his place in the school's counterculture. I couldn't see how I could help Shawn, and I lost track of him after he left the school.

If I had only had an out gay teacher I read again.

I knew what kids were going through, yet I was silent. Sure, I spoke up for gay kids, but in the most profound way I could have helped them, just by being visible, I closed my eyes. I never helped other boys like me escape from the humiliation in the shower room.

It was Shawn who finally moved me to speak.

Right then and there, in bed and in the dark, I made the decision to come out at school. The next few weeks, I told a few close colleagues I knew well. They were unwavering in their support. But how could I come out to the rest of the faculty and staff? I couldn't have conversations with every person on campus.

I decided to come out at a faculty meeting, a forum for self-disclosure that today seems a bit sensational. But I knew so few teachers who had come out that I had few models, little protocol. I found a promising context in an upcoming faculty discussion about the teaching of gay and lesbian issues at our school.

The morning of the faculty meeting, I was petrified. My deep fear was not about job security; it was about self-exposure. I was nervous about the Catholics on the faculty, the older and seemingly more traditional teachers, culturally conservative African Americans, colleagues with their hidden stories: those with closeted gay spouses or who were closeted themselves, those who were questioning their sexuality, those touched by AIDS.

Before the meeting, the faculty gathered in front of the red climbing structure in the lower school for the yearbook photo. I smiled, but my heart was racing, my stomach tightening. It was a cool October afternoon, my favorite time of year. I would have done anything to stay outside and skip the vote. But it was time to leave the playground, to face who I was, to face years of shame and guilt by ridding myself of my secret.

It was time to be visible.

We convened in a circle in the Music Room, a large, comforting space with walls of wood and very large windows. The room was very much a children's room. Colorful musical instruments on the walls. Binders stuffed with songs on shelves. A blackboard with a musical scale and labeled notes

I was the first to speak when the discussion opened; I wanted to get it all over with. I breathed deeply; my hands and voice shook. I talked about my first day of school and how I found out I was different in the recess yard with the boys. I described the next few years, sitting on the sidelines, occasionally playing jump rope with the girls and paying the price of ridicule for doing so. That was the dilemma of being gay in the sixties: was it better to be alone or to have female friends, ensuring the boys would then make you the butt of jokes?

I looked up at my colleagues, some of whom are leaning forward, quietly encouraging me along. The teacher next to me began to cry. I tried not to look at her, plowing through the rest of my talk so quickly I wondered if anyone could understand what I was saying. I ended with the story of Shawn Hughes. Some teachers gasped. I paused, feeling the emotion rise within me. I worried that if I began to cry, I would lose control and not be able to continue. I spoke as forcefully as I could with a plea that we begin to teach about gay and lesbian people so that children – *all* children – would be able to tell their stories.

I left the meeting shaken, scooting out the back door before I could make eye contact with anyone. I sat in the driver's seat, clenching my hands. What just happened? I felt like I'd had too much to drink at a party and was now trying to piece together what the hell I'd said and done.

I closed my eyes at every stoplight. I felt like I'd put an enormous speaker on the roof of my car that announced that I was gay, complete with music by the Village People in the background: "YMCA," "Macho Man," "In the Navy."

I called my best friend, Ed, who lived a few floors above me in the apartment building. Ed, at sixty or so, was twenty-five years older than I was, but still ranked among the younger residents of this building filled with elderly residents. He suggested we go out to dinner at Club Café, a gay restaurant in Boston's South End.

I began to relax at the restaurant, surrounded by gay men. My anxiety began to abate; here I didn't have to worry about what people here thought of me. Everyone seemed so confident. People knew who they were, didn't hide who they were, and liked who they were. No dramatic announcements were needed.

I slept well that night, but I woke up the next morning in a panic. Today there would be the eye-to-eye contact, the *what should I say to them* awkwardness. But the morning began well. On my desk was a bouquet of flowers from a colleague with a note that read: *To help you celebrate.* Then a heart. Then the name *Anne.*

I was still smiling when the Latin teacher, a man who had been at Shady Hill for some thirty years and was, to my knowledge, a devout Catholic, came into my classroom. He was the only teacher in the school who wore a sports jacket and tie every single day.

"That was quite a wonderful thing you did yesterday," he said. "It was very courageous and moving."

I now knew the day would be good.

And it was. An African American teacher soon stood outside the window of my classroom and, near tears, reached through and grabbed my arm. "Wow," he said. "I don't know what to say." By recess, my mailbox was filled with cards and notes of support, not just *good job* messages, but thoughtful, right-on-target expressions of what had happened yesterday.

The novelty of my coming out slowly ebbed. I began to feel safer, calmer. I felt better about myself. What I didn't fully realize at the time was how essential my coming out to the community was to my future, my ability to love.

CHAPTER FIVE

ONE STEP, TWO STEP

Dr. Martin Luther King, Jr., once said, "The arc of the moral universe is long, but it bends toward justice." Before the Massachusetts SJC even heard the arguments from the plaintiffs in the *Goodridge* case, the arc had started to bend, at least a little. A few years earlier Vermont had begun granting civil unions to gay couples. They weren't marriages and they weren't equal to marriages, but they were a step in the right direction. For the first time in the United States, the government had granted formal recognition to gay couples.

There were subtle bends in the arc as well. Many of these were cultural rather than legal steps forward, such as the decision by *The New York Times* in 2002 to print same-sex commitment ceremonies along with straight marriages under the heading *Weddings/Celebrations*. Gay relationships were finally deemed worthy of being among the "news that's fit to print."

I remember waiting for *The Times* the Sunday morning of the first same-sex commitment announcements. I looked out the window of our living room two or three times to see if it had come yet. When it did, with a thud from having flown over fifteen stairs before it hit our front door, I brought the paper in, sat on the sofa with Bruce, and opened to what used to the *Styles* section. There, with so many other straight couples, was the announcement for a partnership and the civil union ceremony to be held that day in Vermont. *The Times,* it was a changin'. And it was doing so because the country was changing. Howell Haines, the executive editor of *The Times,* had said as much when he announced the newspaper's decision to include announcements of gay and lesbian unions: "In making this change we acknowledge the newsworthiness of a growing and visible trend in society toward public celebrations by gay and lesbian couples – celebrations important to many of our readers, their families, and their friends."

Bruce and I began to read about Daniel Andrew Gross and Steven Goldstein, the two men whose commitment ceremony was announced that morning in the *Times.* They were to have a ceremony of civil union in Vermont that afternoon. Mr. Gross worked for GE Capital in Stamford, CT; Mr. Goldstein for Attention America, a consulting firm he founded. The announcement even went into the details of their dating history. They met each other through the personal ads when Steven answered Daniel's witty description of himself as a '"Nice Jewish boy, 5 feet 8 inches, 22, funny, well-read, dilettantish, self-deprecating, Ivy League, the kind of boy Mom fantasized about." When Daniel visited his parents at Thanksgiving and informed them that the name of his new love was Steven, his mother simply replied, "Oy."

The story in the *Times* that morning wasn't just two strangers' story; it was also our own. Sure, the Goldstein/Gross announcement didn't match our romantic history perfectly, but that morning we just enjoyed the simple idea that two men were in the weddings section. That one similarity made the story ours.

There were specifics in their announcement, most strikingly how Daniel and Steven met. Like the two of them, Bruce and I met through the personal ads, although our first date wasn't facilitated through the Internet. On-line dating hadn't quite taken off in the mid-nineties, so one of the only alternatives to the bar scene was putting an ad in the newspaper.

I didn't summon the courage to put an ad in the paper for at least a year after I came out to my therapist. It took me months to even enter a gay establishment. I didn't know what to expect. I hadn't been taught the ways of the gay world and felt more like a teenager waiting to attend his first school dance than a thirty-something adult who had been *teaching* those teenagers for over a decade.

I remember driving around and around the block where Arlington Street Church stood across from the Boston Commons.

Why couldn't I go inside?

Why had I done this every Saturday night for over a month and a half?

Inside, I'd read in *Bay Windows*, gay people were dancing. Perfectly safe, the announcement said. No drinking. No smoking. And lots of line dances to boot: you didn't even have to dance *with* someone if you didn't want to.

Still, I drove around again.

Finally, I parked a block away, got out of my car, and walked to the church. I stood near the door for about ten minutes, inching myself closer, then backing away.

I'd come out to the entire school. I'd told my friends. I'd come out to my therapist. I'd come out to myself.

Or had I really? That was the only reason I could think of that was keeping me paralyzed outside the church door. I'd said the words, but this was where it got real. Where I might meet someone who'd ask me on a date. Where I might meet someone whom I might want to ask on a date.

I turned around and headed back to the car and drove home. I called Ed.

"I don't know what's wrong with me," I said. "Why am I so scared?"

"You'll do it some night," Ed said. "Don't put so much pressure on yourself. You'll do it when you're ready."

I wasn't ready the following week. I drove to Boston, circled the church, parked, stood near the door, closer this time, and tried to peak inside. I couldn't see anything, but I heard music. Mary Chapin Carpenter was singing "Passionate Kisses."

I returned the following week. I hung out at the door. Did anyone recognize me by now? This was silly. I just had to walk up one step, two steps, open a door, and there I'd be. I'd be happy. I'd be relieved.

But when I did walk those steps, when I did open the door, the relief was like nothing I'd ever felt before. I looked down at about fifty men dancing. The sight overwhelmed me. I had no idea what emotion I was feeling; I only knew that I had no room to feel anything but this emotion.

A table was set up at the top of three steps that led to the dance floor, which was nothing more than a church basement, complete with poles that the men expertly avoided as they danced.

"That's five dollars." The man behind the table was in his seventies, decades older than most of the men in the room, and his back was hunched from a broken vertebrae. He wore a plaid flannel shirt and jeans. He put my five dollars into a tin box, then handed me a nametag and a marker.

"Welcome," he said. "You're new, aren't you?"

"Very."

I stayed at the top of the steps for a minute, watching the crowd. Then, suddenly, a man approached me, and took my hand without asking. He was a handsome, thirty-something man in tight jeans with muscular arms.

"I really don't know how to dance," I said. "I'm new."

"I know," he said. "I've never seen you here before." I smiled, taken aback that he noticed me so quickly. "It's easy. It's just a two-step. Follow me."

I watched his feet, which seemed to be taking many more than two steps at a time. "Keep at it," he encouraged.

I did. Miraculously, we finished the dance. I wasn't sure what to do next. Was I supposed to hang around him for another? Thank him and wait for another invitation?

Instead, I blurted, "You know, when I said I was new, I really meant new. New to all of this. I'm just coming out. This is my first time at a gay *anything*, not just a gay two-stepping dance."

The man smiled, but I could tell he was disappointed. He wanted more experience, someone he wouldn't have to teach later in the evening. "Well, welcome to the family," he said, but then walked away.

Maybe I should have felt bad: I'd been dropped like the proverbial hot potato. But I felt anything but. That this man might have had other designs on me, that he might have wanted to dance the night away then go back to his apartment, filled me with confidence.

Unless, of course, I was making this all up. Maybe he was just disappointed in my dancing ability and wanted to find the cowboy equivalent of Barishnikov. *Who cares? I'm here.* Another man asked me to dance. I was slightly disappointed when he told me he was moving to San Francisco in two weeks.

Wait a minute. You're here to dance with men for the first time, not to find a soul mate.

I danced a few times more, but mostly I watched. The room was filled with gay urban cowboys, many dressed in ornate boots and wearing cowboy hats that they occasionally tipped at the end of a dance. The lights dimmed for the last dance, a slow one. The men paired up and made their way around the circle to Anne Murray's "Could I Have This Dance?" After all the years watching straight couples dance and kiss and hold each other; after *When Harry Met Sally* and *The Way We Were* and *Annie Hall* and *The Philadelphia Story*; after the hundreds of TV shows like *Father Knows Best* and *Cheers* and *The Cosby Show* and *Love Boat*; and even commercials with their perfect hetero couples flushing their troubles down the toilet drain; after song after song like "When a Man Loves a Woman"; after Tracy and Hepburn, Rhett and Scarlet, Jack and Jackie O, and Fred and Ginger; after chaperoning countless high school dances and proms; and finally after my own failed foray into straight romance: now, suddenly, I realized I'd been living in translation all these years, as if my life had been one giant paraphrase.

That night I decided it was time to start learning my native tongue.

I went Saturday after Saturday. It became the focus of my week. After the dance, a group of us would head to Napoleon's, a gay piano bar about a block away. We'd drink and talk. We didn't cruise the place for available men. We really did just talk, Napoleon's being one of the few gay bars in the city where the noise level allowed conversation.

I loved going to the bar with a group of gay men, feeling that I was one of the guys, my type of guys. But I was also just coming out. I wanted a boyfriend. I wanted to go on dates and spend romantic Saturday mornings waking up in another man's apartment. My desires went far beyond just sex, but I hadn't really envisioned a shared life with someone. At least not yet, although I knew I wanted that eventually. I took out five or six *The Boston Phoenix*. The last one read:

GWM, 37, 5'10", thin, br/br, professional,
good-looking, romantic, sensitive, caring,
into film, fitness, books, writing, music,
theater, fun, seeks similar man 30-42 for
friendship/more. Box 1238

This ad was better than the one I had written shortly after my introduction to two stepping, when I first started to date. I had learned that unless you included the words "good looking," guys envisioned you as Quasimodo. "Into fitness" meant you weighed less than 300 pounds. "Friendship first" was just another way to draw the line at first-date orgies. Still, this latest ad was perfectly dull compared to others that included measurements of not only height but endowment (surely these guys had mistaken centimeters for inches) along with references to preferred sexual positions. Lesbian ads, on the other hand, cited the search for life partners whose interests included gardening and spirituality.

I was new to all this, and my learning curve in the fine art of meeting men through the newspaper had been long and slow. One of my first dates was with a guy who assumed I'd be a partner in an S & M session; I'd understood the words "I can be gentle" to be a character trait rather than a sexual attitude. Naively, I agreed to meet him at his house for dinner even though I'd never laid eyes on him. My nerves were not calmed by the words of a friend of mine who told me in all seriousness not to worry because "you're far more likely to be killed by a homophobic psychopath if you bring a guy back to your place. At his place, he has to deal with what to do with the body."

Bob was a hulking, balding thirty-something man with a gruff voice and sunken eyes. Dinner consisted of cold cuts and potato chips, a meal to be consumed quickly so that we could get to the real meat of the evening, which Bob slyly referred to as "a little rough and tumble." I pled asthma problems and left after the ham sandwich.

A few weeks later I had lunch with a guy whose passion in life was erotic gargoyles. Another met me in Harvard Square, but instead of our planned walk around the Charles River, he took me to Kinko's Copies so he could photocopy dozens of bird feet drawings for a presentation he was giving on the West Coast later that week. Still later, a man asked me to meet him at a coffee shop in Boston. When I didn't recognize him, he introduced himself to me. He'd said he was forty but he was clearly in his sixties. When I asked him if he wanted to step inside the coffee shop – our agreement, after all – he refused, informing me he had brought his own coffee in a thermos as well as a screenplay he wanted me to read right then and there. The most recent guy to answer my ad confidently told me that I'd take one look at him and say "*Ahhh!*" I met him at a seafood restaurant where the bathroom doors were labeled "buoys" and "gulls." This was my one laugh of the night.

I was tired and skeptical when a guy named Bruce answered my ad on a Sunday evening in late August. The ad was to expire the next day, and I almost didn't check my phone messages at *The Boston Phoenix* that one last time. But I did, and I answered Bruce's message to me at his voice mail box at the newspaper, giving him my home telephone number. We talked briefly when he called an hour or so later. We decided to meet for lunch on Tuesday in front of Wordsworth, a bookstore in Harvard Square, then we'd eat in a small Caribbean restaurant across the street.

"Look for a guy in purple high tops," I told Bruce. "You can't miss me."

He didn't. He was on his way to the bank when he spotted my sneakers, then called me to join him. Bruce's ease told me that this little detour was a simple cash withdrawal, not some lengthy transaction that would take as long as photocopying birds. I didn't know what this date would turn out to be, but it did feel like the first *normal* date I'd had.

The lunch went well, so we decided to take a walk along the Charles River. I learned that Bruce worked for an investment firm that

Sentence missing advised nonprofit organizations. He was recently divorced from a woman with whom he had remained close friends. Charlotte, the youngest, had been born while he was at Dartmouth's Business School. Shortly after her birth, Bruce came out. He was relieved that I didn't walk the other way after he talked about his children.

"The minute I tell a guy I have kids, it's usually the last I see of him," he said. "But you said in your voice message at the newspaper that you really liked children, so I figured I was safe with you."

He was right to trust me; I *did* love kids, and knew that I would love to have one of my own someday, even if I had to do it alone, although gay adoption was still relatively rare in 1995. I wondered if I'd ever meet Bruce's daughters, if we'd make it that far.

That weekend we had our second date, dinner and a movie, *Smoke*, a low-key slice of life comedy that was my cinematic staple. I loved novels and films where seemingly nothing happens, perhaps because of my inability to follow plots. Bruce was relieved there was no violence. He had a great aversion to it on the screen, he explained to me as I drove him to his studio sublet in Somerville. The images replayed over and over in his mind and he had a hard time sleeping.

I pulled up in front of Bruce's apartment building, double parked, and wondered if he'd kiss me on the cheek or suggest we meet again sometime. I thought of the wonderful scene in *Manhattan* when Woody Allen and Diane Keaton are walking down the streets of New York early on their first date. He stops abruptly and suggests they kiss that very minute to avoid the *should we kiss* tension at the end of the evening. If the two just do it, he explains, it'll be done with and they won't think about the dreaded moment of decision when they say goodbye.

Such good advice, I thought.

"Would you like to come up for some tea?" Bruce asked.

Not a beer. Not a glass of wine. But tea. I loved that he felt confident enough to offer tea. So easy. So safe. Earl Grey is hardly a prelude to a romantic evening, I thought.

I was wrong.

Our courtship was hardly extraordinary: more and more dinners together, sweet messages left on answering machines, the first overnight, the meeting of the parents – Bruce's, that is. He had warned me that his mother and father couldn't go through an entire evening without fighting. He liked to tell the story of their trial separation and subsequent reconciliation. They decided to fly to Hawaii and renew vows at the foot of a mountain, which they later discovered to be a dormant volcano. The night I met them their hostility for each other was anything but dormant. The first image I have of them is his mother slapping his father across the head because he didn't say hello quickly enough to Bruce and me when we entered the restaurant and found them waiting at the bar.

But the oddest moment was when I met Bruce's ex-wife in late fall.

"Beth would like to meet you," Bruce said one Saturday afternoon in my apartment.

"Great," I said "When?"

"In a about half an hour. She's on her way with the girls from Carlisle."

"Okay," I said, immediately checking what I was wearing. It was like I was going on another first date. "What are we going to do?"

"Lunch in Harvard Square," Bruce said. "Then maybe we'll do a little shopping."

"Let me change my clothes."

"Honey, you look fine. We're not going anywhere fancy. It's just an informal lunch."

Hey wait a minute, I thought. Isn't this how you and I met? An informal lunch in Harvard Square? Isn't this getting a little too weird?

When Beth pulled up in her decade-old Volvo wagon, she was wearing a fur coat. Beth was from Savannah. Maybe this was Southern informal, I thought, even as I wondered why anyone would need a fur coat in Savannah.

I put my hand on the back seat door, ready to sit with Kate and Charlotte, who was in a car seat.

"Come on up front," Beth said, a Southern lilt in her voice. She was an attractive woman, with short blond hair and creamy skin. "Bruce, you sit in the back."

It was beginning to feel like a party, with our congenial hostess arranging the table setting so that we were all able to get to know just the right people. The fall afternoon was cold but it was very warm in the car.

"Volvo has the best heaters," Bruce said from the back seat. "If you want a good heater, buy a car that's made where it's really cold."

This was the small talk of a nervous man.

"Maybe some introductions are in order, Bruce," Beth said as she put on her sunglasses, made a U-turn, and headed toward Harvard Square.

"Right," Bruce said. "Girls, this is my friend Ken."

Before Bruce had a chance to introduce his daughters by name, Charlotte, blurted a huge, "Hi, Ken," then giggled as she shoved her pacifier back in her mouth.

"This is Charlotte," Bruce said.

"Hi, Charlotte," I said, trying to match her enthusiasm without sounding over-the-top.

"And this is Kate."

Kate's hello was eager, yet crisp, decidedly different from Charlotte's; she was setting herself apart from her younger sister. She reached and pulled the pacifier out of Charlotte's mouth.

"You're too old for this," she said. "*I* dropped my pacifier when I was eighteen months and you're over two years old."

Charlotte began to wail.

"Girls," Beth called without anger but with a singsong lilt that I suspected didn't vary one fraction of a note whenever she had to referee. "Be good to each other until we get to the restaurant. Bruce, why don't you move in between them?"

Bruce hopped over Kate to separate the two. The car was quiet for a few seconds.

"Stop it," Kate said.

"What's wrong now?" Bruce asked.

"Charlotte's looking out *my window*," Kate complained. "Tell her to stop."

"I don't think we can tell her where to look, Kate," Bruce said.

"But it's *my* window."

"Kate once complained that Charlotte was breathing *her air*," Beth said.

We ate at a kid-friendly restaurant in Harvard Square, right next door to where Bruce and I had our first lunch date. The kids ordered pizza; the adults ordered salads. Beth asked me questions about teaching. I found out that she was a history major, had a brother nine years her junior, missed the South on occasion, and noted that the winters in Boston couldn't match those in Hanover, New Hampshire, where she and the girls lived with Bruce while he was in business school.

No bumps. Amazing. I was beginning to understand that the spontaneity of the meeting was keeping us all from becoming too nervous, from anticipating what could go wrong, from rehearsing what we should and shouldn't say. I was also beginning to understand Beth a little. She wasn't easily flustered. She was a religious woman (an Episcopalian) and I wondered if her wider view of the world allowed her to keep what could be seen as tragic events in perspective. Still, how did you keep this perspective when your husband has come out after ten years of marriage?

After lunch we visited a few stores, including Funny Farm, a novelty toy store that much to the girls' delight sold a pig that pooped jellybeans.

"Stocking stuffer," Beth whispered to Bruce.

And then, just as suddenly as it began, the meeting ended. The girls got tired; Charlotte started to cry because she wasn't allowed to have all the sweets she wanted at a candy store. Bruce had to drag her out to the sidewalk, quite literally kicking and screaming. But Kate wanted to hold my hand. We walked with her parents back to the parking garage.

And that was it. No awkward moments. No hostility. No lines drawn in the sand.

Later that night, after Bruce had talked to Beth on the phone, I asked him what she thought of the day.

"She says I got it right," Bruce said. "Do you want to go to their place for Thanksgiving dinner?"

Not long after I met Beth, Bruce and I rented an apartment together a few blocks away from where I was living. The lease on Bruce's sublet had run out, and he either needed to find a new place on his own or find one with me. We had very little discussion about living together; it just seemed *right* even though we had only met a few months earlier. The move was an enormous change for me. I hadn't lived with anyone since my sophomore year in college.

We fell in love with the first apartment we saw: a one-bedroom with a sunroom and a back porch overlooking a tiny yard. Our landlady, a seventy-something woman who at first seemed leery of living below two gay guys in her duplex, nonetheless offered us the place through the real estate agent who had introduced us to her. Bruce later told me that gay men have a great reputation in the rental market: no kids and obsessively neat.

If Helen didn't notice the disarray in our apartment when she came upstairs one morning to ask us to shovel the snow, then Kate and Charlotte's first sleepover surely put an end to the myth that gay men were perfect tenants. It was a disaster. Kate was at her most pugnacious, and Charlotte's *laissez-faire* attitude only irked her even more. There were loud fights over macaroni and cheese (*You gave her more than you gave me!*) and which television station to watch. Kate announced that there was no way she and Charlotte were going to bed at the same time; there had to be at least a half hour between lights out for her and lights out for her much younger sister. The evening ended in a screaming, stomping, and crying match, with Charlotte smashing Kate's snow globe against the wall, an event that eventually was a multisession therapy topic for Kate.

Despite our not living up to her expectations, Helen grew to be quite fond of us, and we grew to see her less as a landlady and more as a neighbor. We discovered that she really wasn't quite as straight-laced as she appeared. On her living room wall was a small rack intended to hold miniature spoons from around the world, only she had displayed swizzle sticks embossed with the names of different bars she'd visited around the country. She was hard of hearing, and we learned to tolerate her early evening routine of watching reruns of *Love Boat* at full volume while she sipped her highball. By that summer, we had been invited to her 75th birthday party held at the local VFW hall, and when she became ill with cancer shortly after we moved out of the apartment, she called us to her bedside two days before she died to say goodbye.

Helen was the first person Bruce and I had grown to know as a couple. Everyone else we knew had histories with one of us. So far I'd blended into his circle of friends and he into mine without much difficulty, but we both knew that all of these friends held an allegiance to the one of us they'd known first. Helen treated us as a couple so matter-of-factly that when she referred to us as "the boys upstairs" to her son and daughter-in-law, there was an implicit understanding that these boys were a couple, not just a pair of roommates.

Someone once told me that as you grow older, you become more of who you've always been. I think you could say the same thing about living with someone. I'm not sure Bruce and I necessarily learned anything earth shatteringly *new* about each other in our apartment; we just saw more of those qualities that we loved or tolerated when we had our separate places. I discovered that Bruce snored *every single night*, not just those nights we had spent together before permanently sharing a bed. And he learned that I didn't just shrink my own clothes when I ineptly did my wash; I shrunk his as well when we joined laundry.

Bruce always knew I was a sensitive guy, but I'm not sure he completely understood how easily I could find a cloud wrapped around the most silvery of linings. I have the remarkable ability to find a subtext under subtext under subtext for every noun, verb, and even preposition that comes out of his mouth. My half-joking response to a simple line like, "Ken, you've been working so hard today. Why don't you just relax on the back porch and read for a while? I'll finish up here in the kitchen," would be, "I think you meant 'back porch' metaphorically. You want me on the back porch *of your life*. You know, if you want to end our relationship, you can just be honest with me."

I soon discovered that Bruce wasn't only late for our dates, he was late for just about everything, while I, on the other hand, proved equally annoying with my belief that arriving anytime after fifteen minutes early was, in fact, inexcusably tardy.

Of the two of us, I'm the one who looks more long-term while Bruce thinks in detail. I'm the driver for lengthy trips to Vermont, but no one can parallel park like Bruce. He can tell me which laptop computer is the better bargain and then head straight for the checkout line of Best Buy, but I'm the one who reminds him that it doesn't matter how much it costs because we have enormous car and fuel bills to pay at the end of the month. Oh, and didn't we just buy a new laptop last week?

One Memorial Day weekend, we'd decided to have a few people to the apartment for a mid-afternoon lunch. My job was to run the errands and bring home flowers, French bread, a bottle of wine, napkins. I was also to buy a new CD to provide some background music to the affair, even though in combining our collections, we'd had over 500 of them. I told Bruce that I'd be back in about two hours.

When I returned, I immediately noticed that the hardwood floor was still dusty, clothes were still strewn over the furniture, and books were left opened next to the living room chairs. And with all our CD's now spread out over the floor in front of our stereo system, the apartment had become *messier* since I'd left. Bruce sat cross-legged on the floor, reading the cover notes to Cheryl Wheeler's latest release. He didn't seem to notice me as I walked in.

"Um...Bruce?" I said. "What are you doing? I thought you were planning to clean the apartment."

When Bruce looked up, he appeared as if he'd been woken up. "Oh, hi, Honey. I am cleaning. Right now I'm alphabetizing the CD's. I'm on the W's. I'm almost done."

Alphabetizing the CD's? Of course! None of our guests would notice the pigsty in front of them! They'd be too impressed with how the arrangement of our CD collection could rival Tower Records.

We adjusted. We took life one step at a time. We grew to understand that we often *do* become more of who we are as we get older, for better and for worse, and that while our relationship certainly changed our lives, it wasn't going to be a rip tide that carried us away from our true selves.

And we learned that this was a very good thing.

CHAPTER SIX

CROSSROADS

By October of 2003, the Massachusetts SJC was four months late in releasing a decision on the *Goodridge* case. The waiting seemed endless for me; I could only imagine how hard it must have been for the plaintiff couples that had been living with this case for over two years now. During this waiting period the legislature was dealing with gay marriage through a task force that sought to reach a compromise on the issue such as Vermont-style civil unions for gay couple, while opponents of any sort of same-sex unions were feverishly working to introduce a constitutional amendment, whatever the ruling of the SJC.

Perhaps United States Representative John Lewis, a veteran of the Civil Rights Movement, described the national mood best when he said, "From time to time, America comes to a crossroads with confusion and controversy. It's hard to spot that moment. We need cool heads, warm hearts, and America's core principles to cleanse away the distractions. We are now at such a crossroads over same-sex couples' freedom to marry."

"Crossroads" was certainly a perfect word to describe where Massachusetts was. And it wasn't just a political or historic crossroads where many same-sex couples found themselves. There was possibly a brand new crossroads to consider – whether or not to marry.

Deciding to get married, of course, had never been the crossroads for gay couples as it has been for straight couples, although there were many other rights of passage we shared: the first overnight, introductions to friends, exchanging apartment keys, sharing an apartment, exchanging rings. By 2000, Bruce and I could put a check next to all these items on the relational to-do list except for one: exchanging rings. It was time.

We had discussed the possibility of a commitment ceremony shortly after we moved in to our apartment in 1996, but we were not well off financially and could hardly go to our relatives for support. Our rent was cheap but our salaries were low and Bruce's business school loans were high. We decided to save our money for our house and skip the commitment ceremony, opting instead to privately exchange rings in the living room of our apartment.

Since marriage was unavailable to us, we'd already selected an anniversary date from a list of brainstormed possibilities. The date of our first meeting? The date we expressed our love for each other? The date we moved in together? We finally went with the date of our first meeting, August 29th. And so on that date five years later, we exchanged the rings.

We'd ordered the rings a few weeks earlier at a small jewelry store that had a reputation for treating gay couples respectfully. Finding businesses that were friendly to gay people had become second nature to me since I'd come out; I knew where I was welcome and where I was barely tolerated. We didn't buy an appliance from the store where we saw two clerks roll their eyes and laugh at us while we were checking out a new dryer, then never ask if they could help us.

The jeweler where we purchased the rings was perfect, neither bludgeoning us with cloying enthusiasm nor letting us wander off on our own. Bruce ordered a rose gold band with a coin edge, while I chose a simple white gold one with subtle imperfections to make it look handmade. I liked that my ring looked worn; it seemed right for the marking of a relationship that had already lasted five years.

Bruce picked the rings up at the jeweler's in Cambridge on the way home from work the day of our anniversary.

"I've got them," he said.

"Let me see."

He took the boxes out of the bag and opened one up. The packaging seemed like a nesting doll: a bag, a box, then another box, then a small, soft bag, and then *voilà:* the ring. "This one is yours."

I snatched the box from his hands and studied the band. "Wow. This is really nice." I slipped the ring on my finger.

"Wait a minute," Bruce said. "You can't put your own ring on. We need to give them *to each other.*"

"Oh," I said. "I've never done this before."

"I don't have a lot of experience either. But I do know we should put them on each other. That's the whole point, Ken."

We sat down on the sofa that we'd bought together when we moved in – our first joint purchase. I returned my ring to Bruce; he gave his to me.

"Which hand?" I asked.

I thought of the song by Martha Reeves and the Vandellas: *Third finger, left hand/that's where he placed the wedding band.* So clear. The placement of a wedding ring in heterosexual relationships hardly requires discussion. Not so for gay couples. Where you wear your ring carries social and political significance. Do we wear the rings on our third finger left hand and try to pass as straight? Do we wear the rings on this same finger for a different message: to announce that we are just as legitimate as straight couples? Do we go for the right hand to signify our union while at the same time indicating that we're gay? Do we go for the right hand, middle finger, as a friend of mine did, announcing our union with an implicit "fuck you" to those who were offended by her relationship? Do we both have to choose the same finger?

Because Bruce worked a great deal in Texas, we talked about wearing the ring on our left hand, just like any other married couple. This would certainly make it easier to deal with general conservatism of the state and some of the boards he advised. This was before the Lawrence decision. Gay sex was still *illegal* in Texas at the time. People would assume he was a straight married man. But what would he say when he was asked questions about his wife? Up to this point he'd managed to deal with questions about his private life without lying. References to "my better half" or "my spouse" allowed him to avoid what might have been a career-damaging revelation while still being honest to our relationship.

"I think we should go with the right hand," Bruce finally said. "Let them think what they want to think."

"Are you sure?"

"Yes, I'm sure. Look, people in the know will understand what the ring on the right hand means. Everyone else will just be a little confused."

He slipped the ring on my finger; I slipped the other on his. I held my hand in front of me, splaying my fingers to highlight the ring.

"I love it," I said.

I've come to view that moment when we exchanged rings as far more courageous than I considered it at the time. Here we were, two men alone in our apartment, privately pledging to do what our government said we couldn't. We were at our own crossroads, deciding whether or not to play along with the government and ignore any formal recognition of our relationship, or taking the emotional and symbolic plunge, despite all the messages that we wouldn't last, that what we were doing was somehow abnormal, and that our relationship was one giant moth, ready to eat away at the fabric of society.

We decided to trust our hearts. We did it. We wore each other's rings. We thought this was as far as we'd be able to go, that our private exchange was, in fact, our wedding.

Not so, said the Massachusetts SJC.

CHAPTER SEVEN

PROPOSALS

The SJC handed down its ruling the week before Thanksgiving break, a time when eighth graders are typically both antsy and tired, eager to leave school for vacation yet aware that this is the last Thanksgiving of their Shady Hill career, which for some began at four years old. I planned a mock Constitutional Convention to keep them focused that week, and had given them first period that Tuesday for some final preparation and research about the delegates each of them would portray. They were off to math by 9:30 a.m., and I was sitting at my desk to correct some papers when the phone rang.

"Something really important is happening," the woman's voice said. "The SJC just granted full marriage rights."

I recognized the voice as Maureen's. She was president of the Unitarian Universalist Church Bruce and I attended. We had been working together on church business so much lately that her number was now on my speed dial.

I asked Maureen to repeat what she said.

"Full marriage rights. I'm watching it on the news right now. They broke in with a special report."

"You mean a few rights but they'll call it something else, right?"

Maureen was a staunch "straight ally" and unequivocal supporter of marriage rights for gays and lesbians. Perhaps her passion for the issue had clouded her understanding of what had really happened.

"That's not what it sounds like," she said. "I'm looking at the TV right now. There's a special report. It says right at the bottom of the screen that the court has granted marriage rights."

I still wasn't convinced. As we had learned when Vermont granted civil unions, "marriage rights" didn't necessarily mean it. I still suspected that the court had ordered the creation of some sort of parallel institution. I was willing to believe that Massachusetts would offer "marriage lite," but not the real deal.

Maureen was insistent. "Hold on," she said. "Let's listen to this." I could hear the TV voices in the background, but couldn't make out the words. "I'm telling you, Ken," she said, "it's marriage. That's exactly what the reporters are saying."

"Unbelievable," I said, an odd choice of words since I was finally beginning to believe her. "Wow, Maureen. I'll never forget where I was or who told me this news. You're burnt into my mind forever."

"Isn't this amazing?" Maureen said.

I hung up the phone and immediately went on line to see the decision myself. I read that the vote was close, with four justices siding with the plaintiffs and three siding with the state, but that didn't matter. In the words of Chief Justice Margaret Marshall, the oldest constitution in the United States "affirms the dignity and equality of all individuals" and "forbids the creation of second-class citizens." She then quoted the *Lawrence* decision, writing that "our obligation is to define the liberty of all, not to mandate our own moral code." The seven couples that had been battling the state for years could now legally marry in Massachusetts.

That Marshall would use language that spoke to the heart as well as the mind did not surprise those who knew her well. A native white South African, she grew up under apartheid. As a foreign student in the early 1970's, she traveled across the United States urging people to endorse economic sanctions against her native country. And her native country heard her: she was barred from ever returning to South Africa because of her political activism. Her majority opinion revealed a jurist who understood the toll injustice takes on the disenfranchised. "The marriage ban works a deep and scarring hardship on the community for no rational reason," she wrote. For those critics who pointed to child rearing as the *sine qua non* of marriage, Marshall noted that "the task of child-rearing for same-sex couples is made infinitely harder by their status as outsiders to the marriage laws." In other words, if we are truly concerned about the role of child rearing in the institution of marriage, we should make it easier, not harder, to raise children.

Justice John M. Greaney, in a concurring opinion, not only echoed Marshall's words but spoke directly to the public when he wrote, "I am hopeful that our decision will be accepted by those thoughtful citizens who believe that same-sex marriage should not be approved by the State. I am not referring here to acceptance in the sense of grudging acknowledgment of the court's authority to adjudicate the matter. My hope is more liberating." He went on to describe the "common humanity" we share and the "principles of decency" that should guide us toward full acceptance. He ended his opinion with the very words Mary Bonauto had used in her arguments to the SJC in March. We should extend the right of marriage "because it is the right thing to do."

I was hit with a rush of pure adrenaline that masked some of the subtler emotions that pulled beneath the surface. I was happy, certainly; I could now marry my partner of ten years. I told myself our marriage would be better than the ones we both had seen our parents struggle through, more honest than the one Bruce had with a woman before he understood his sexuality. But then some doubts began to gnaw at me: What if he *didn't* want to marry? We had both eagerly awaited the decision but hadn't spoken specifically about what it meant for us. What if he'd become too skeptical after ending his previous marriage? What if his parents' tumultuous marriage had made him too jaded to make that "'til death do us part" pledge? Maybe the wills we had recently drafted and the rings we'd exchanged in private were enough for him. And maybe *I* would get cold feet once I thought long and hard about what marriage had meant for my own mother and father and so many other couples I knew. I had to acknowledge that I knew of very few good marriages.

And then there were the political questions. The summer and fall had shown us that this was going to be the beginning of a long battle. Only minutes after the decision was released, the Internet was flooded with statements from same-sex marriage opponents. President Bush interrupted a state visit to England to denounce the ruling, stating that "marriage is a sacred institution between a man and a woman" and that the Massachusetts ruling "violates this important principle." He pledged he would work with Congress to eliminate the possibility of same-sex marriage once and for all. Massachusetts Governor Mitt Romney had already called a news conference in front of the State House to declare that marriage must remain between one man and one woman, since "it has been so since the beginning of time." He pledged his support for a state constitutional amendment banning same-sex marriage. This from the man who once tried to convince the electorate that he'd be a better advocate for gays and lesbians than Ted Kennedy.

Was it worth getting my hopes up so soon? Shouldn't I wait until the issue was decided – *truly* decided beyond any doubt – before imagining Bruce and me in matching tuxedoes as we tied the knot at our church?

But right now, I needed to get in touch with Bruce. He'd left for Texas on Monday on a business trip and was staying in the small apartment his firm had rented for him for his frequent trips to Dallas. He wouldn't be there now; he was most likely meeting with a client or reporting to a finance committee of some board.

I decided to e-mail him. *GREAT NEWS* I wrote in subject line. *MASS COURT GAVE US FULL MARRIAGE RIGHTS. NOT CIVIL UNIONS. FULL MARRIAGE RIGHTS. CALL ME. LOVE YOU. K*

I stared at the screen until my students trickled in. I gathered them into the meeting area of our classroom. "Since you're right in the middle of studying the US Constitution," I said, "you should know about a ruling that the Massachusetts SJC just handed down. It fits right into what we've been talking about."

I explained what had happened. The kids asked questions about the difference between the US Constitution and Massachusetts law. They wanted to know if the ruling meant that gay people could get married anywhere in the United States. They talked about the equal protection clause, *Brown v. Board of Education*, the difference between a civil marriage and a religious one. They asked me when people could start to get married. They wondered aloud which of the gay people they knew might marry.

"So what about you, Mr. H. Are you going to get married?"

I loved that the kids were so comfortable with my being gay, but as a rule I never discussed my private life with them beyond movies Bruce and I saw. I have a stock response for personal questions I don't want to answer. I tell the kids that it's completely okay to be curious and to ask questions, but that sometimes people might not want to answer those questions. We have to respect people's privacy if they ask for it.

But that answer didn't seem right today. And besides, I really didn't even have an answer for them.

"We'll see," I finally said. "At least now I can, right?"

Now I can. Can: such a tiny word, known grammatically as a helping verb.

What an understatement.

I can marry. I never would have believed that I could say this thirty, twenty, even ten years ago.

That evening, I settled in front of the TV with Oscar and Shakespeare, our two basset hounds, at my feet. I switched channels from local coverage to CNN to NECN (New England Cable Network) to the national network news. The emotional ride of watching the reporting and interviews – one minute marriage seemed a sure thing, the next minute there was sobering talk of loopholes in the ruling – was merely a rehearsal for the ride many of us would take over the next months and years.

As I got up to feed the dogs, Bruce called from his cell phone. He'd read my e-mail that told him about the decision but hadn't heard anything else. I updated him on what I'd heard on TV. Having been a lawyer earlier in his career, he had a sharper legal eye than I did. It all sounded quite positive, he said, but his voice was hesitant. Neither of us said anything for a moment. Shouldn't one of us at least bring up the subject of our own possible marriage, even if to agree that we'd talk about it later? If we'd been a straight couple, we would have had a wedding years ago. But we weren't straight, and now with the possibility of marriage before us, I had no idea what the protocol was. If we *did* want to marry, who should ask whom?

Bruce explained that he had to catch a flight to Austin so he could be on time for a breakfast meeting in the morning. If he checked into the hotel before 11:00 p.m. my time, he'd call; otherwise, we'd talk again tomorrow. I would have offered to stay up later for a marriage proposal but decided not to get my hopes up. *I love you*, we both said before we hung up.

I stayed up past 11:00 p.m. anyway, doing anything to keep me busy since I was unable to construct a mental fence to keep my thoughts about marriage neatly contained. I had to stop thinking about it altogether if I wanted to get any sleep at all that night. I corrected papers and played with the dogs. I did a wash. I surfed the net for news other than the marriage decision. I cleaned my attic office. I reviewed old bank statements.

The phone rang at about 11:30 p.m.

"Am I calling too late?" Bruce asked. "We sat on the runway in Dallas for about an hour. Thunderstorms."

"Don't worry. I was still up. I haven't even let the dogs out yet."

"Oh, good."

I asked him a few perfunctory questions about his day. His meetings had gone well but he was tired and a little worried about his 8:00 a.m. meeting tomorrow with a money manager who was having problems.

"It looks like they're going to fight this SJC decision," I said. "Tonight Romney said he's going to try to amend the Massachusetts Constitution if the SJC doesn't give him any wriggle room to institute some form of domestic partnership instead of marriage."

There was a pause. Bruce tends to think more carefully than I do before he speaks, and I had become accustomed to the occasional silences over the phone when he and I would talk. But tonight the silence seemed even longer than usual. I didn't know what to say next about the SJC decision without making it personal, and I wasn't sure this personal conversation should happen over the phone.

Bruce broke the silence.

"Will you marry me?" he asked.

"Of course I will," I said, relieved at the break in the tension.

"Wow," he said. "Who'd have ever thought this would happen?"

"Not me."

Now legally and officially, we would be recognized as a couple. There would now be a written evidence of our relationship.

We would have our own recorded history.

The headline of *The Boston Globe* the next morning was huge: *Gays have right to marry, SJC says in historic ruling*. Every other story on the front page, save for a short piece on a runway controversy at Logan Airport, was about the decision. In the middle of the page was a color photo of a glowing gay male couple with their son at a celebration of the decision at the Old South Meeting House.

To my colleagues at school that day, I would show nothing but pure elation at the news. Everyone else on campus was overjoyed; shouldn't I, of all people, feel the same way? It would seem downright ungrateful for me to quibble on this momentous day. None of us at school could have ever foreseen such progress only a few years ago. But the day had come and I was deeply moved, certainly, but I also had to acknowledge I was angry and resentful and frightened, too.

Although I'd come to accept my years in the closet as not being lost time, I sometimes wanted those years back, every last one of them, and the front-page photo of the young gay couple and their son brought this home to me again. The photo touched me; it was, after all, rare to see gay men portrayed so positively on the front page of a major newspaper. I had always wanted to be a father, but grew up believing it was impossible for two men to create a family with children. Now not only was this possible, the SJC had stated that this was a *right*. I wondered what my life might have been like if this decision had come down when I was coming of age.

I was also angry and afraid. In the newspaper that morning were the stories of dissent, ominous signs that gay people might become political pawns at best and victims of violence at worst. Backlash was not something my sympathetic straight friends considered that day, but I did. According to *The Globe*, Republican strategists had reacted "with glee" to the ruling, despite their very public dismay. We were approaching a presidential election year, and here was the issue to firm up the Midwest and the South.

The arguments against gay marriage from such groups as the Massachusetts Catholic Conference and the Massachusetts Family Institute were similar to the reasons presented during the Vermont debate. Biblical teachings were at the core, even though Jesus had not said one word about homosexuality. Warnings were issued about the end of the social order as we knew it. The usual litany of perversions was repeated over and over: incest, bestiality, and pedophilia would soon be legal in your hometown! You'd have expected entire baseball teams to unite in orgiastic bliss with their underage batboys and furry mascots.

I entered the classroom, my plan book tucked under my arm. We always discussed major news stories, so I couldn't very well avoid addressing the marriage issue again with the kids. I was ready to give as thoughtful and as balanced a lesson as I could. As I was about to speak, I realized that this class, this very moment, was one of the toughest in over twenty years of teaching. I'd spent all fall with these fifteen students trying to teach them the value of inclusion. How was I supposed to explain Governor Romney's response to the SJC ruling in light of these questions? I was always trying to help my students look within themselves to discover, in Justice Greany and Mary Bonauto's words, "the right thing to do" in their treatment of people. I believed that the Governor had acted in direct contradiction to what I'd been teaching.

I also believed that Romney's "over my dead body" speech minutes after the ruling would someday be seen as a "George Wallace moment" – standing in front of the school house doors, barring entrance. I was certain that once gay marriage was accepted – and there was no doubt in my mind that it would be, even if many years from now – Romney would be seen as an obstructionist to civil rights. Would the kids remember that I had refused to take a stand on this day?

Part of my struggle was in trying to understand the difference between my values and my political opinion. While inclusion of all sorts was a value I wanted all my students to learn, I usually shied away from stating my political beliefs, hoping that my neutrality would make it safer for my students to state their own. But when did a value become a political stance?

I made an uneasy peace with myself and began my lesson the morning after the SJC decision. I asked the students to talk about *the facts* of the case. I explained that I didn't want to hear what they *felt* about the decision; I wanted to hear what the *knew* about it. There would be plenty of time for opinion sharing later.

The thought bubble in my mind said: *This is all bullshit. They know how I feel. Would it be so unprofessional of me to tell them? Why are you putting yourself back in a closet? If this were a civil rights case based on race, you'd have no problem at all expressing your point of view.*

But this wasn't about race, it was about being gay, and whatever I said to the kids would be seen in light of who I was. I didn't want them to link the issue to me.

My request that they stick to the facts of the case lasted all of a minute and a half. Cassie told the class how her mother hung up on a John Kerry for President campaign call last night because he refused to endorse the SJC ruling. Ryan found his seat in time to decry Mitt Romney's response. *Can you believe it? He's evil. Why does he care if two guys get married?*

"Wait," I said. "I need to know that you understand this case before you offer an opinion." I didn't want them to repeat last night's dinner table conversation without thinking carefully about what they said. If they were going to criticize Romney and his allies, they needed to do more than parrot their parents.

So I pushed, even as I still felt inauthentic, a bit of a traitor for not using this opportunity to rally support around a cause. I explained that the SJC gave the legislature 180 days to respond to the ruling and that many legislators – along with many legal experts – interpreted the 180-day waiting period as merely a time for the state to update their marriage applications to reflect the new reality. There would be no more references to husband and wife. Town clerks would also need training to deal with the new definition of marriage. Then in 180 days the first applications for marriage licenses would be accepted from gay couples.

I could barely keep from smiling when I said the word *marriage*. The normalcy of the vocabulary was in and of itself soothing. As a linguist, I was fascinated by what certain words *represented* for people. The word *house* surely prompted a different mental image for students from the wealthier suburbs of Boston than it did from, say, kids from the barrios of New York City. I mentioned this idea to the class, wondering aloud if the words *married couple* might someday prompt an image in our minds of two women or two men instead of merely a man and a woman. It would probably depend on one's exposure, we decided, and exposure, we all knew, had a great deal to do with the media. In May, when gay couples were allowed to marry, perhaps we'd see images of newlyweds that would broaden our spectrum of visual possibilities. These pictures might help bring to our imagination a far wider range of it.

"Yeah," Cassie said. "You've got to see it. Then you start to change your mind."

"It's like 'show me the money,'" said Ryan.

They were right. Seeing is believing, and we had half a year to go before we'd see any wedding pictures in the newspaper.

I was exhausted and emotionally raw as I sat in my classroom at the end of the day. I couldn't imagine what it must have been like to teach at a school where the consensus was that the SJC was wrong. I wanted to be pleased with the way I'd handled the class discussion about gay marriage, but a nagging voice kept telling me that I should have been more direct, let the kids know how I really felt. What were they thinking about a gay teacher who refused to show his own emotions on such a momentous day, especially when their straight teachers had been quite open about their feelings on the ruling?

I was also tired from giving my opinion to every teacher who asked it. I grew weary saying the same line over and over again. *Yes, I'm happy, but I'm concerned about backlash. It really is amazing, though, isn't it?*

It's too bad Bill Weld isn't still governor. Then we'd have somebody at the top on our side.

I didn't want to answer any more questions about whether Bruce and I would marry. Even though he had asked me, we hadn't set a date. We hadn't even *seen* each other since we'd decided. It still seemed premature to announce our engagement, a word that seemed all wrong for a couple who had been together for so long. We'd been engaged in our relationship for years now. Using that word to describe our future plans sounded like a step backwards.

I was beginning to understand that no matter how private I'd been with my relationship with Bruce, this decision opened up that relationship to public comment and inquiry. It didn't matter that I thought this was unfair. It made no difference if I envied that my straight friends could keep their relationships as private as they wanted to. The gay marriage news was big, and because we were a gay couple, we were part of that news. We were taking another step toward visibility.

I shut my classroom door for some peace and quiet. At my desk I saw that Bruce had e-mailed me around noon. He told me that his breakfast meeting went fine and that he was on his way back to Dallas where he would call from his apartment. He didn't mention anything about the ruling, but I assumed he was getting a very different reaction in Texas. I had the luxury of listening to National Public Radio while Bruce's options were probably Dr. Laura and Rush Limbaugh.

At home that night I played with Oscar and Shakespeare, both of whom the right wing would have labeled scarred for life if Bruce and I married. I flopped on the sofa to watch the news. A full day after the ruling, gay marriage wasn't just the *top* story, it seemed to be the *only* story. After about five minutes, I turned the TV off. I couldn't watch any more bickering about the right to marry. I couldn't even watch politicians on my side try to convince the public that "gay people are people, just like you and me." It was terribly draining, even degrading, to watch myself being defended on TV.

When Bruce called, he was quiet.

"Are you doing all right?" I asked.

"I'm just tired," he said. "I really want to get off this treadmill and stop traveling. It's exhausting."

Still, I sensed something else was on his mind.

"Are you happy you proposed to me last night?" I asked.

"Yes," Bruce said.

"Yes, but?"

"No. Just yes."

"I'm glad, too," I said.

"I'm glad you're glad," Bruce said. "I knew you wouldn't propose to me, so I'm glad I took the leap."

"Why do you say that?"

"It's okay, Honey. Really. It's just that you're a little more cautious than I am. You're the introvert. I'm willing to take risks."

He was right, of course. I was the more hesitant in love. But I wasn't convinced that I wouldn't have proposed to him.

"Bruce?" I said. "Would you marry me?"

"Of course I will," he said.

CHAPTER EIGHT

BATTLE LINES

Voices on both sides of the debate grew louder the weeks after the SJC decision. Archbishop O'Malley, along with the bishops of the dioceses of Worcester, issued a statement calling the SJC ruling "a national tragedy." O'Malley ordered the statement to be read at all masses over one weekend, although many parishes simply left copies of the statement in the back of the church for those who wanted to read it. Other priests read the statement without comment as part of announcements. Some priests were clearly torn by O'Malley's order, citing gay and lesbian parishioners who were an integral part of their churches. One priest said that the statement was "hard to fathom" in light of recent church scandals. A few weeks later, the church would follow up its statement with a glossy million-dollar mailing urging voters to push for a ban of gay marriage, even though by law the church would not be required to perform weddings for same-sex couples. When I heard about the mailing I couldn't help but wonder why the church didn't do a million-dollar mailing on child abuse.

One of the greatests threats to marriage equality came in the form of a new organization of political and religious leaders, the Coalition for Marriage, whose goal was to end the debate once and for all by changing the Massachusetts Constitution, permanently barring gays and lesbians from marrying. The group, which included leaders of the anti-abortion movement, met on the State House steps in January, promising to take the issue to the airwaves and door-to-door. The group was essential in organizing a petition drive to put the issue of marriage on the ballot. According to the Massachusetts Constitution, once the required number of signatures was gathered, then only 25% of the legislature needed to support the referendum at two Constitutional Conventions, held two years in a row. The threshold was low.

Other opponents to gay marriage posed the possibility of civil unions to the Massachusetts SJC shortly following its November decision. On February 4th, the SJC released an advisory opinion that left no doubt that only marriage would satisfy its November 18th decision, saying that civil unions were "an unconstitutional, inferior, and discriminatory status for same-sex couples." The state had to issue marriage licenses to gay couples starting on May 17th, 2004.

The timing of the SJC advisory opinion was important, since the legislature was scheduled to hold a constitutional convention on February 11th to begin the process of amending the state constitution. The Sunday before the convention, 2,000 opponents of gay marriage rallied on the Boston Common. A group of past and present office holders addressed the gathering, designed to pressure undecided lawmakers into supporting the ban.

I received an email the night before the rally, urging me to attend the counter-demonstration on the steps of St. Paul's, the gay-supportive Episcopal cathedral across from the Boston Common. With such short notice we couldn't begin to match the numbers of Catholic protesters, but at least we'd get a little news coverage along with them.

I thought there would be no question that I would go and that Bruce would go with me. I printed the e-mail announcement and handed it to him at dinner.

"We should go to this," I said.

Bruce paused. I could tell he was rehearsing what to say.

"I'm really busy tomorrow," he said. "Remember, I'm leaving for Texas on Monday. But you go for both of us, okay?"

I wanted to scream *Don't you know how important this is! Our very marriage rests on what these people are doing to stop us. We have to go.* But I didn't. Bruce had always been respectful of my decisions – political and otherwise – and I wanted to do the same.

"Are you sure?" I said. "You can go for an hour or so and then head back. It won't take up that much time."

"I don't think so," Bruce said. His voice was soft, sad. I knew he was unhappy about his constant traveling, but his demeanor suggested something deeper.

"What's wrong?" I asked.

Bruce said nothing but began to clear off the table. He stood at the sink, rinsing plates, shoving leftovers down the garbage disposal instead of saving them for Oscar and Shakespeare as he usually did. I stood behind him.

"Talk to me," I said.

He turned around. He didn't bother drying himself and his hands were dripping.

"It's too hard for me," he said. "I can't invest so much of myself just to have the whole thing taken away. I feel like I'm setting myself up for this huge disappointment. There's no question I want to spend the rest of my life with you. I'm 100% certain about that. But I can't get my hopes up right now that we'll be able to get married. Who knows what will happen between now and May?"

"But you *want* to get married, right?"

"Yes," Bruce said. "I very much want to get married. And I hope we do. But emotionally I just can't dwell on that too much right now. So go. You go to the rally tomorrow. I'll stay here and do some work for my trip on Monday. I'll be with you in spirit."

The next morning after church, I took the train into Boston. I felt extremely lonely riding by myself. I looked around me, wondering how many people on the train were planning to attend the rally. I did what I knew I shouldn't have done: I tried to guess, through appearances alone, who might be going into Boston to protest gay marriage. I couldn't help it. Anyone who looked remotely conservative became the opposition, the ones who, for reasons I couldn't fathom, were threatened by Bruce and me marrying.

I was wrong, of course, and knew in my head, if not my heart, that most of the people on the train didn't even know that the rally was taking place. They got off at Chestnut Hill, Kenmore Square, Copley: all stops before Park Street, where the crowd was assembling. I walked up the subway stairs into the cold, overcast day, and immediately looked to the Common where a huge swarm of people had gathered, many bearing signs too far away to read. A platform had been erected where Cardinal Sean O'Malley and Former Boston Mayor Flynn were to speak.

When I looked at the church steps where we were supposed to meet, I only saw a handful of people. My heart sank. *This is it?* I thought. *They've got thousands and we're supposed to counter them with twenty-five?* Along the Common were lines of buses that had transported hundreds of people after mass.

I went into a Dunkin Donuts for some coffee to warm myself. It was packed. I grew despondent as I listened to snippets of conversation. *Do you remember when Sister Anne taught sixth grade? I heard Father Carlton was going to retire next year. The Sodality's going to do something other than a raffle this year to make money.* There was no antigay language in the donut shop. Just fifteen or so people small talking before they waged war on an issue that affected my life profoundly. Maybe that was the scariest part. These were not rabid right-wingers spewing hate, at least not overtly so. These were people who would travel for an hour to stop two people from legally sharing their lives together, get back on the bus and talk about the upcoming Red Sox season or who was going to run for Parish Council, then have dinner with their families. Trying to make the government abide by their religious beliefs had become second nature.

These were the people I had grown up with in Lynn. They were my mother and father, my aunts and uncles, my friends' mothers and fathers; for all I knew, they were my friends. They could have even been me if I hadn't left. I could have been on one of those buses, with a wife I didn't love enough, trying to convince myself that not wanting to be gay was the same as being straight.

How had I come so far from this world of my youth? I sometimes believed that it was my knowing I was gay at an early age that kept me at arm's length from my family and neighborhood. I knew instinctively that I didn't belong, so I didn't even try. Once I left my family and childhood city, I realized the departure had begun many, many years earlier.

I left the donut shop with my coffee warming my hands. I brought the cup to my lips, sipped, then pressed it against my cheek. The heat comforted me; I kept the cup close to my face as I approached the Common, where the crowd had become more strident. Hoisted high were signs with the familiar quote from Leviticus about homosexuality being an abomination. Never mind that the Bible also forbade the eating of shellfish; it was this line that the religious right had seized upon to justify their prejudices. Other signs read *Adam and Eve not Adam and Steve!* and *Man + Woman + Children = Family* and *Gays Will Burn in Hell,* complete with red and orange flames.

I remembered the book about Catholicism my father gave me. I pictured the devil, the piping hot oven in his dental laboratory, my father warning me that hell was even hotter. *You will end up here if you don't behave.* These lessons were now being taught to a new generation of children, both gay and straight, who had accompanied their parents and churches to the rally. And these children – some as young as ten or eleven – were holding signs that condemned others to hell. I found this most disturbing of all.

I have always loved Viola's opening line from *Twelfth Night.* After she is shipwrecked on an island, she appears on the stage with a captain and sailors and asks, "What country, friends, is this?" I love its simplicity, the inherent contradiction of calling these nameless men "friends" while not having the slightest idea where she is. It at once reveals her extraordinary alienation and yet her capacity for intimacy.

I felt as if I were on a foreign shore that day, yet these were people I had known intimately growing up.

What country *was* this?

As Cardinal O'Malley approached the podium, I looked around at the signs. Homosexuality as mortal sin. Homosexuality as the downfall of civilization. Homosexuality as illness. The word *illness* was particularly poignant for me. I remembered the night I watched the Miss America Pageant. I remembered the tattered white medical dictionary. The definition of homosexuality. The word *illness*. The possibility of a cure through electric shocks. *Please don't let them attach those wires to me.* Years later, the tape still ran in my mind: *you're sick.*

I left for the steps of St. Paul's while O'Malley was still speaking and the numbers were still swelling on the Common. More and more people had begun to gather at our counter-demonstration as well. I joined the crowd. It was clear that we did not have the organization of the Catholic Church's protest across the street, but the pro-gay marriage people were spirited. I felt at home.

I read these new signs around me, the ones that supported my cause. Most urged people to let others love whom they loved; others warned of the dangers of writing discrimination into the Massachusetts Constitution. But the man standing next to me held a very different sign: MY PEDOPHILE PRIEST CAN LEGALLY MARRY. The men nearby congratulated him on being so daring. They exchanged sympathetic hugs. They had been there too, they said. They believed completely that the church had seized upon the gay marriage issue to divert attention from the sex scandal that still loomed over Catholic clergy.

A celebratory mood had begun to envelop the crowd. In front of me an elderly couple – he in a tweed wool blazer and khakis and she in a turtleneck sweater – stood holding hands. They appeared to be a quintessential Boston brahmin couple. I wondered what brought them here. Was it a son or daughter? Grandchild? Were they political activists who wanted to do good in the world?

Suddenly the man began to sing and his wife joined him.

We shall overcome. We shall overcome. We shall overcome someday.

They sang it as if they had sung it many times before. I'd sung this song many, many times at Shady Hill, especially at our annual Black History Assembly. I loved the song and found it moving. But at that moment, as the rest of the protesters added their voices, I felt that I understood the song for the first time. When I sang the words *deep in my heart, I do believe*, they came from deep in my heart. My eyes began to well at the purity of the voices, the quietly adamant tone of the angry men who had been touched by the sign condemning the Catholic Church.

I wished Bruce were with me to share this moment. I had to remind myself that it was better for him not to be here, even if it wasn't better for me.

After the song, a black woman stood before the crowd to lead us in other protest songs of the sixties: *We Shall Not Be Moved. If I Had a Hammer.* The crowd chanted *What do we want? Equality! When do we want it? Now!*

It was about this time that Ray Flynn took the stage on the Boston Common. I tried to ignore him and the cheers he was eliciting from the crowd. We all continued singing and shouting. A middle-aged woman crossed the street and headed toward us, her body tight and her jaw clenched. She arrived at the steps just as we had finished a song.

"Do you mind?" she asked, her voice quivering with anger. "You are interrupting our rally. We can't hear. It is *rude*."

Well, that's the point, lady, I thought.

She marched across the street to her cadre of fellow parishioners, who nodded their heads in appreciation of what she had done. I imagined them egging her on only a few minutes earlier, when she suggested she might give those people across the street a piece of her mind. *Yes! Do it! You shouldn't be afraid of them.* The scene was reminiscent of the social dynamic of junior high, when cliques of kids would consolidate their power into one or two intimidating representatives.

But we ignored the woman, and kept singing and chanting until the protest was over, even though we were greatly outnumbered.

I was both energized and disheartened on the train back home. I was a child of the apathetic mid-seventies and had never been to a political rally before even though I'd always been politically engaged and had my degree in government. I was beginning to realize that the value of a protest wasn't just in bringing attention to a political stance; it was also individually empowering. I was reminded of what my psychiatrist had told me over and over again during years of therapy: *you aren't powerless...you can take some action...you don't have to be silent.*

Still, whatever psychological benefits I'd reaped from the afternoon were tempered by the images I took with me of those children holding signs and aping their parents' bigotry. I thought it ironic that while the right wing often accused gay people of "recruiting" or "indoctrinating" children into acceptance of homosexuality, there were no children on the steps of St. Paul's. On the Common, however, children were once again being carefully taught, as I had been, to fear gay people.

My enthusiasm was also tempered by my solo appearance at the rally. By the time I got home, Bruce had finished his preparations for his Dallas trip in the morning and was in his red gym shorts and tee shirt, having just returned from the health club. I didn't know how much I should talk about my afternoon. I gave him some of the basics: the scene in the donut shop, the "pedophile priest" sign, the appearance of Ray Flynn and Sean O'Malley, and, finally, the presence of the young people during the Catholic Church's rally. Bruce nodded and added, "that's interesting" a few times, but I could tell the conversation was disturbing for him, so I backed off.

"You have to believe me when I say that I want to keep an emotional distance from the politics of all this," he said. "But I don't want to keep an emotional distance from you."

"Of course," I said. "I just need to keep remembering that."

I thought of another Shakespearean line, the one that Cordelia, King Lear's daughter, says at the beginning of the play after her two sisters have insincerely professed their love to Lear. Cordelia, who loves her father more deeply than any of his daughters, can't measure up to her sisters' flattery.

"What should Cordelia say?" she asks quietly.

She loves her father; she doesn't feel the need to prove it. Her silence is not the absence of love. It is filled with love. Yet Lear, in a tragic moment, won't trust her love unless she resorts to her sisters' hyperbole.

What should Cordelia say?

What else did I want Bruce to say?

I should have come with you. I love you so much that I should have overcome my fears just to be with you.

No, that's not it. That's not the way relationships work. If we start setting up hurdles, we'll only set them higher and higher until no one could possibly leap to such heights.

"I love you," Bruce said.

"I love you, too."

"Look," he said. "Let's not make my political distance personal. Let's not make that about us."

"Okay," I said. "I'll try."

When I arrived at school the next day, not many people had heard about the rally on Sunday. When they asked me how my weekend was, I varied my answer from "fine" and "too short, of course" to a more detailed description of the events. I hadn't slept well the previous night, so as I sat at my desk at the rear of my classroom, I didn't engage in my usual banter with my students as they trickled in before the official start of the day. I worked at my computer, eavesdropping on the truncated retelling of the weekend: a ballet performance, two DVD's in a row at a friend's house, snowboarding in Vermont, a "lame" dance at a nearby school. In a funny throwback to the fifties, one girl's mother had hosted what sounded like a Tupperware Party for cosmetics. "I was with all these old ladies," said Angela. "Well maybe not *old*, old. Anyway, they kept trying to put make-up on each other as they drank more and more wine. It got pretty funny."

After having taught for over twenty years and meeting thousands of teachers in my career, I realized I was witnessing a moment that not all teachers get to experience. These kids *wanted* to be at school this Monday morning. They were happy and laughing, completely at home. When I finally walked to the meeting area at 8:20, it took me a few minutes to get the kids' attention.

"Focus, everyone, focus," I urged.

"Wow. I saw *50 First Dates*, too. Wasn't that hilarious?"

"So my friend Walter from camp? He ends up flying off the snowboard and jamming his wrist into a tree. He almost broke it."

"I want to learn how to snowboard."

"Anybody see any other movies?"

I cleared my voice theatrically. "One person at a time, please. Please stop talking."

No luck. The conversation grew louder and more chaotic. I finally walked to my desk and grabbed the large brass bell I generally only used outside to bring the kids in after recess. I rang it five or six times in the room. The sound was deafening.

"Jeez, Mr. Harvey," said Ryan. "You don't have to go all military on us."

"At least you're quiet now," I said. I reviewed the day's schedule with them, reminded them of the rehearsal for *Strike Up the Band* at 2:30 p.m., went over the list of jobs for the week.

"Did you have a good weekend, Mr. Harvey?" Cassie asked.

Yet another reason to appreciate these kids, I knew. How many eighth graders are even remotely interested in what their teacher does over the weekend? I looked at my class as they sprawled out on the futon or sat five on a two-seater sofa. This was the class that didn't laugh for a second when I showed them a photo of a butch-looking Willa Cather while we were reading *My Ántonia*. When I had asked these kids which character they'd most like to have as a friend from *Lord of the Flies*, they picked Piggy, the asthmatic, effeminate outcast of the group.

I thought of the kids I had seen yesterday, each with their signs, their parents encouraging them. I thought about how frightened I would have been to go into that crowd. It was my junior high years, all over again. It would be like standing in the shower. Yet here, with these kids, I felt safe.

"My weekend was okay," I said. I thought about giving them a few details of the protest yesterday, but it was getting late and math class started soon. So I just smiled and added, "but it's really great to be back with you guys."

CHAPTER NINE

CALL TO ORDER

A flurry of activity descended upon the Massachusetts State House the days before the Constitutional Convention. With great fanfare, opponents of same-sex marriage arrived with boxes of letters supporting the constitutional amendment. Sons and daughters of gay and lesbian parents showed up at the door of the Senate Majority leader, Robert Travaglini, a Democrat who, along with the Speaker of the House, opposed gay marriage. As the petitioners waited, they chanted in opposition to a woman who held up a newspaper ad that suggested children of gay and lesbian parents were socially deprived.

Although according to the Massachusetts Constitution the earliest date for a state wide referendum on gay marriage was in 2006, some advocates were beginning to worry that Governor Romney would find a way to prevent gay marriages before then. I shared that fear. When asked right before the convention whether he would block the Department of Public Health from ever granting marriage licenses to gay couples, Romney said that he "would follow through with the law of the state as it exists at the time." His words prompted speculation that he would try to somehow change existing law, although there appeared to be no legal way of doing so before May 17th, the date established by the SJC for the first gay marriages. Mary Bonauto called Romney's words "slippery" and warned, "It's one thing for the governor to state his views, but it's another for a governor to use the power of his office to obstruct a court ruling."

For now, however, both sides of the debate focused on persuading lawmakers before the upcoming Constitutional Convention. Legislators' voicemail boxes were filled to capacity, e-mails flooded their computers, their phones never stopped ringing, and it was difficult for a legislator to walk down the halls of the State House without being accosted by one side or the other. The language was getting more and more strident. Bishop Gilbert Thompson of New Covenant Christ Church remarked, "To say there is such a thing as a gay Christian is saying there's an honest thief." But perhaps the most biting criticism of gay marriage came from a Black minister who had traveled from his native South. At a news conference he stated that he would join forces with the Ku Klux Klan if it meant defeating gay marriage. I found his words were all the more shocking since every African American legislator – along with the major African American newspaper columnists – were unequivocal in their support for marriage equality.

On the day the Constitutional Convention opened, I headed to the State House as soon as my last student left school. I took the subway from Harvard Square to Park Street, pretending to read *The New York Times* I had bought at the kiosk. I couldn't concentrate. I closed my eyes, trying a few relaxation techniques I'd learned over the years but that had never worked. How do you actually think of *nothing*? As soon as my mind seemed clear, someone would show up, clanging about in my head as if digging through a cabinet of pans and metal bowls.

At the State House, it was clear that today was not going to be a replay of Sunday's rally. TV reception discs sitting on top of enormously high cranes hovered over the State House steps. Today both sides of the debate were evenly matched, and there was no clear line separating the two. People were arguing with each other, staring each other down, waving signs. HOMOSEXUALS ARE POSSESSED BY DEMONS and JESUS IS LORD. The message was the same: SAVE OUR CHILDREN. I'd like to say that these signs pained me, that I was deeply saddened by what children were learning from this propaganda, but right then I wasn't. I was absolutely furious, pure and simple.

I saw a pro-gay marriage sign against a tree that I picked up. Its owner ordered me to put the sign down. He thought I was a member of the opposition, ready to destroy his words. "I'm on your side," I said to his relief. I felt like a soldier in a war movie, climbing out of a smoldering bunker, hands raised, begging not to be shot as the enemy.

I knew the day would be heated and that no "call to order" inside the building was going to ease the tension out here.

It was impossible to get into the legislative chamber that day because people had lined up so early in the morning to get a seat. A two-hour line had formed around the building to enter and wait in the halls. I stayed outside, wandering throughout the crowd, when I saw two young men holding hands. I missed Bruce. I wanted him home from Texas, in my time zone, in my immediate orbit.

I finally attached myself to a group that was chanting "no discrimination in the Constitution." I believed in what I was shouting, but I knew I was holding back. I didn't want to be the loudest voice in the crowd, the one who stood out. I stood in the rear, sometimes yelling and sometimes just mouthing, then moved on to another group. What was my hesitancy about? Why did I feel little like that boy in the schoolyard on his first day of school watching the other boys play dodge ball? These were people on my side, people like me. Well, sort of. These were young gay college students, they were people in their sixties and seventies who, if they weren't gay themselves, I imagined were the supportive parents and grandparents of gay children, PFLAG (Parents and Friends of Lesbians and Gays) members. A sad truth: many gay men of my generation had died.

So I felt both welcomed and out of place, the forty-something gay man, walking about alone, both eager and reticent to claim my voice in the crowd. It wasn't in me to wave signs at cars or yell at the woman holding the crucifix. So I struck a tacit bargain with those around me: *I'll let you be in the spotlight, I'll let you be the ones on TV with your voices and your signs, if I can just stand in the back and copy you.* I gave myself permission to just be present, to not feel obligated to lead the march or even strike up conversations with those on my side of the issue. I wouldn't have known whom to speak to anyway. With my khakis, button-down shirt, dark green overcoat and leather gloves, I looked downright nerdy compared to the young people with brilliant scarves and secondhand chic coats. They had come of age just as the tide was shifting toward gay people. They were confident, not concerned with politeness, not only speaking out but expecting to be heard. I felt like they had come to demonstrate for gay rights while I was waiting for the formal lecture on the topic.

"This is ridiculous," I heard behind me. "Next thing you know, they'll be letting you marry your grandmother."

The man, with a stubbled chin and smoking a cigarette, was talking to me. I didn't know what to say, so I looked away from him.

One of the young women who had been chanting spoke to the man.

"Hey, if you want to marry your grandmother, you go right ahead," she said. "Personally, I think it's sort of weird."

"No," the man said, this time louder and more guttural. "You're the one that's gonna make it so people end up marrying their grandmothers."

"I plan to marry my girlfriend," the woman said. "You can marry whoever you want. But your grandmother? That seems a little unnatural to me."

The man started muttering something about having sex with other relatives, but the young woman smiled at him until he ran out of steam. He walked away.

"That was impressive," I told the woman. "I'd never have thought to say that."

"You just can't let them get to you," she said. "If you do, you'll never make it through this whole thing."

We heard on the radio that debate was heated inside the Legislature's Chamber. When one legislator went into a diatribe about how the "Lord is our defense and the Holy One in Israel is our king," I started to seethe. I tried to remember the advice from the young woman who had spoken so calmly to the man with the grandmother obsession, but this free associative speech seemed to reveal nothing but deep-seated bigotry against gay people. Between the legislator's ranting of "let's not reward bad behavior" and her waxing about the arrival of the Pilgrims, I had to take deep breaths. Even some people on her side had to be rolling their eyes at her bizarre outburst. Perhaps she might even do her side more harm than good.

Hearing proponents of gay marriage both calmed and moved me. Dianne Wilkerson, an African American state senator, tearfully recounted her life growing up in the segregated South. "I was born in my grandmother's house in a shotgun shack in Arkansas," she said. "The public hospital did not allow blacks to deliver children. We lived in constant fear of the Ku Klux Klan. Blacks had to pull off the road for whites to pass. I had two uncles that decided enough was enough in 1935. . . . It sent one uncle to Springfield, which is how I got there." And then her conclusion, which brought me to the verge of tears: "I can't send anyone to that place from where my family fled. My grandmother would never forgive me."

When the convention resumed the next day, the crowd was bigger, but I arrived earlier, skipping our weekly faculty meeting, and was able to make it into the State House this time if not the Chamber itself. I found a space to sit on the floor of the Great Hall, a long, cavernous room with an arched transparent roof where the flags of all the cities in Massachusetts hung. Closed circuit TVs had been set up so that those of us who couldn't make it into the Chamber could still witness the proceedings live.

It was clear that the crowd in the hall supported gay marriage. As I leaned against the marble wall, I realized that for the first time in my two days at the State House that I felt safe; if violence was going to erupt over the issue – and the tension outside the State House certainly made me think this was a possibility – it wasn't going to happen here.

The speeches inside the Chamber were eloquent and emotional. Lawmakers talked honestly and personally. A Jewish state senator drew parallels between the marriage restrictions proposed to restrictions in Nazi Germany. An Armenian state senator talked about the persecution of her ancestors. The crowd was especially moved when a gay state senator described the night he had to take his adopted son to the emergency ward. He found himself arguing with a nurse over whether or not he was really a parent, since his partner's name was listed as the father on the child's record. Finally, an African American state representative stepped up to the microphone and addressed those black religious leaders who supported the amendment. "Shame on you," he said. He ended by saying that just as we celebrate Massachusetts as the first state without slavery, so too he hoped we would celebrate this day.

When the Constitutional Convention recessed – until March 11th, a date I found interminably far away – I was exhausted from the shouting and singing ("We Shall Not Be Moved" became the relentless theme song of the pro-gay forces), exhausted from my anger, exhausted from being alone with so many people for two days, exhausted from fear. I was also exhausted from reporting to my colleagues at school.

Bruce made his usual nightly call from Texas those first days of the Convention. Sometimes we talked around nine o'clock or so and again right before the first one of us went to bed. These bedtime calls were just for us; we tried to say goodnight without the anxiety of marriage politics hovering over us. But the first call was often just about politics. I'd sum up some of the news stories in *The Boston Globe* and on the local TV news. I'd explain to Bruce what was happening at the State House and how I experienced it. When Bruce expressed concern for my safety during the protests, I assured him I'd be wise and leave if I sensed the beginnings of violence, even while I wondered if, in fact, I would actually fulfill this promise to him. But I understood why he was asking. Bruce reacts swiftly and severely to even the hint of violence. A few weeks after we had met, he showed me a small scar on the palm of his hand. He told me that he had blocked the knife that his father held as he lunged toward Bruce's mother. Bruce caught the knife with his hand. We both had not only worked long and hard in therapy to learn to live with our family histories; we'd also worked with each other.

"Don't you think it's time we set a date?" I suggested to him during one of our long phone calls after the Convention had recessed.

"Maybe we should wait a little longer," he said. "I just have the feeling Romney will try to block the SJC ruling. I don't trust our government to do what's fair."

I reminded him that we needed to talk to our minister, Jane Newman, before she left for Hungary on her six-month sabbatical with her husband.

"You're right," Bruce said.

I suggested August. I knew what I was doing: Bruce's daughters would be in Georgia with their mother visiting their grandparents for the summer. It was how they had spent every summer since I'd known them. Although I got along well with Bruce's ex-wife and his children, I didn't want to rock the boat. Marrying while the girls were away would ensure the peace.

"That doesn't give us much time," Bruce said.

"Much time for what?"

"Well, there's the caterer, the hall, the music, just to name a few details."

"What do you mean, the hall?"

"For the reception," Bruce said. "We can't very well fit everyone into our house."

I was quiet. It was clear we had completely different images of what our wedding would look like.

"I was thinking we might be able to fit everyone in our house," I said. "I figured we'd only invite twenty-five people at the most."

"But the Shady Hill people alone puts the number up to fifty."

"I'm not going to invite everyone," I said. "Just a handful. If we invite any more than that then, yes, we'd have to invite almost everyone."

"What about the people at church? So many have worked so hard for this day, it seems insensitive not to ask them."

I had to agree with him there. But our church had over seventy-five active members. We couldn't afford to invite them all. I found myself feeling sad that we were disagreeing on our wedding day before we'd even set a date until I realized that *all* couples argue about wedding plans. Suddenly, we seemed the most normal couple in the world.

"Look," I said to Bruce, "let's just set the date so we can talk to Jane. Then we'll worry about the details, okay?"

"Okay. But August is really close for a wedding, no matter what the size. Let's push it forward so we can at least keep all our options open."

I thumbed through my calendar on my desk, looking for the long weekends. Bruce was busy with work in October and November, so I ruled out Columbus Day and Veteran's Day. Then came the holidays.

Finally I suggested Martin Luther King, Jr., Day in January. I love winter. I pictured snow and a honeymoon at some cozy bed and breakfast with a fireplace. And I liked the idea of marrying during King's birthday weekend. We could weave some of his words into the ceremony, acknowledging all he had done to pave the way for not just racial equality, but all equality.

Bruce liked the idea. The holiday was celebrated on Monday, January 17th, so we chose Saturday the 15th, King's actual birthday.

Choosing the date proved to be one of the easiest areas of agreement as we planned our wedding. But at least it was a start.

CHAPTER TEN

A STEP BACK

Shortly after the constitutional convention recessed, the issue of same-sex marriage became an even more prominent national issue when President Bush kicked off his reelection campaign by calling upon Congress to begin the process of amending the Federal Constitution. "Decisive and democratic action is needed," he explained, "because attempts to redefine marriage in a single state or city could have serious consequences throughout the country." He went on to say that "the amendment process has addressed many serious matters of national concern, and the preservation of marriage rises to this level of national importance."

I was incredulous, although, of course, I shouldn't have been surprised at all. Still, it boggled the mind that gay marriage – or more specifically Bush's belief that gays and lesbians should be denied this right – was as important to the nation as the abolition of slavery and expanding the right to vote to include African Americans and women. Just as puzzling was Bush's assertion that "activist judges" on the SJC had overreached their decision, even though his very elevation to the presidency depended on far-reaching actions by the US Supreme Court.

Senate Majority Leader Bill Frist was quick to take on Bush's election-year charge for a constitutional amendment, predicting that when same-sex couples started to wed in Massachusetts, "the wildfires will be-gin" and spread to all fifty states. Unfortunately, some well-intentioned politicians from other states fed into this fear. Most prominent was San Francisco Mayor Gavin Newsome, who began issuing marriage licenses to gay couples without the blessing of the courts or the California legis-lature. I found it painful to watch the news reports of gay couples lining up in front of San Francisco City Hall to get their marriage licenses. I strongly believed these marriages would be declared invalid. I also agreed with many gay leaders such as Representative Barney Frank who felt that news broadcasts from the West Coast of illegal gay marriages taking place did not help the cause.

In Massachusetts, it was becoming evident that our side had work to do. A clear majority of legislators had gone on record as oppos-ing gay marriage, twice the percentage needed to send the referendum to the voters. While many of these legislators opposed both marriage and civil unions, a consensus had started to build toward an amendment that banned same-sex marriage but legalized civil unions.

As the gavel came down again in the State House on March 11th, so too did it come down on marriages in San Francisco as a California state court ruled that the same-sex nuptials had to stop. Gay marriage was not, as Senator Frist warned, spreading like wildfire across the country. The real wildfires were the passions on both sides of the debate, passions that became more and more inflamed as the Massachusetts legislature pre-pared to take the issue up once more.

On the evening of March 10th, the day before the Convention was to resume, a candlelight vigil was held in front of the State House in support of gay marriage. Some colleagues of mine at Shady Hill planned to attend, so I went with them.

We boarded the subway to Park Street in Boston and walked to the State House. A few hundred people had already gathered in front of a platform that had been erected for speeches. As we passed candles around, I looked out over the Boston Common. The trees were still bare, the sky gray. People began to sing, but I merely mouthed the words. I was overcome with an enormous sadness right then. We were going to lose tomorrow. I knew it. And Mitt Romney and the Catholic Church were somehow going to prevent marriages from beginning on May 17th. As the evening lit up with candles, I only became more despondent. I felt as if I were at a memorial service.

When a gay activist stood before the microphone and yelled, "How many of you are engaged?" I raised my hand halfheartedly up to my shoulder while others were waving their arms enthusiastically over their heads. I now knew what Bruce had felt like when he didn't want to get his hopes up after the initial court decision.

I don't think any of my straight colleagues noticed my mood as we held our candles. They all seemed too excited about being part of this public support of gay marriage. I loved that they were with me and that they were optimistic, but I also knew they could afford to be. The risk of deep disappointment just wasn't as great for them as it was for me. But this was exactly why I needed them there. I needed to feel optimism beside me, even as I could cynically say to myself that it was easy for them to be upbeat about our chances for victory at the convention.

I didn't teach very well the following day. I walked around the room more than usual, trying to pace away my anxiety. Every chance I had I was at the computer, logging onto *boston.com* where up-to-the-minute breaking news was provided about every half hour or so. I said very little to my students, all the while envying the ease with which many of my colleagues expressed their support for same-sex marriage to their classes. In the building that housed the eighth grade, one teacher even put up a large sign that read NO DISCRIMINATION IN THE CONSTITUTION: SUPPORT EQUAL MARRIAGE on the front door. She'd certainly gone beyond anything I would have dared to do. I loved seeing the sign each morning, but I also dreaded the idea that the community might think that I was the one who had stated my view so openly. I was fearful of the trap that I knew I could easily fall into even in the most liberal of communities. I didn't want my reputation as an openly gay teacher to overshadow my reputation as a good teacher.

And I also felt guilty. Here I was, in what was as close to a perfect work environment as I could reasonably ask for, and I was still feeling isolated, out on a limb. What else did I expect my colleagues to do? A voice inside me kept telling me to count my many blessings, but that didn't keep me from feeling anxious. I wanted to be invisible.

These feelings were especially strong a few days before the convention, when Shady Hill brought in Jarrett Barrios, a gay state senator from Cambridge, and Renee Landers, president of the Massachusetts Bar Association, to discuss the issue of marriage equality with the Middle School. Both speakers were committed supporters who were often in the media during the Constitutional Convention. For thirty minutes the two presented clear legal and moral reasons for same-sex marriage. I knew there were very few schools in the country that would sponsor such a forum and I was reminded again of why I had committed fifteen years to Shady Hill. At the same time, I worried that some kids and parents would see the assembly as just another example of political correctness encouraged by gay people in the community. I left the assembly feeling more uneasy than proud.

I wanted the whole issue to just go away. I didn't want to hear one more time I was deserving of the most basic of rights. I wanted to stop feeling I was somehow responsible for anyone who spoke on my behalf. I wanted summer vacation. I wanted the Constitutional Convention to be over.

I just wanted to get married.

On March 11th, a friend and I left Shady Hill for the resumption of the Convention before school officially ended. By now the subway ride to the State House was becoming routine. As we exited up the stairs at the Park Street Station, we were unexpectedly greeted by our friend Martha, a woman in her early seventies whose 1960's activism had never waned. She was on her way home, having spent the last few hours at the State House.

"It's tense over there," she said. "It doesn't feel good."

She was right. The depth of anger was palpable as we approached the State House and saw the signs, more plentiful and as strident as ever: HOMO IS A SIN and POLYGAMY-INCEST-GAY MARRIAGE, and, my favorite, HOMOSEXUALS ARE POSSESSED BY DEMONS. It was as if the far right had hired the *National Enquirer* to make their signs. Pro-gay-marriage signs were in abundance as well, although the tone wasn't as hostile. One man even managed to keep his sense of humor with a sign that read, WE PLAN YOUR WEDDINGS. WE SHOULD BE ABLE TO HAVE THEM TOO. But for the most part, people were on edge, glaring at each other, arguing with each other, and milling about in the cold, not so much to keep warm as to defy the enemies on a street corner they had claimed, a step to the State House they were calling their own.

An enormous banner hung from the headquarters of the Unitarian Universalist Church, which stood immediately beside the State House. The words CIVIL MARRIAGE IS A CIVIL RIGHT towered over everyone. On the sidewalk below stood two handsome elderly men, each with a hand on the corner of a large sign that read TOGETHER FOR 49 YEARS. They were both smiling broadly; I'm sure they never believed they would even have the possibility of marrying in their lifetime. When they met (in 1956, according to my quick math), they could have been arrested for loving each other. I did some more math, and figured that Bruce and I would have to live to be 94 years old to be together that long.

The crowd continued chanting and yelling as helmeted officers, their guns in full view, walked along the street to stop that one shove that might escalate into pandemonium. If I had kept my promise to Bruce to leave when I thought the situation was dangerous, I should have left right then. But I couldn't. I don't consider myself a brave person at all, but I know I would have stayed there even if violence had broken out. Whether or not I would have allowed myself to be arrested was another matter, but I hoped I'd have the conviction to put my beliefs on the line, even if it meant spending a few hours in jail for civil disobedience. What did I have to lose? What did I *really* have to lose? So many had risked so much more so we could stand in front of the State House that afternoon.

I did move away from the demonstrations when I learned that the State House was prepared for a bigger crowd inside this time. Although the legislative chamber was full, we were told that people could gather in the hallways. Once inside, I could hear a group booming out "My Country 'Tis of Thee." I was worried that the anti-marriage forces had grown in number and that they were, as usual, claiming patriotism as theirs and theirs alone. But as I climbed the stairs, I saw that it was the gay-marriage supporters who were singing. They were as upbeat as ever. I joined them in the back.

On the legislative floor, the political maneuvering was impossible for most of us to follow. One minute we heard the deadlock continued, which would have been a victory for us, and the next minute the news was pessimistic. Ron Crews, President of the Massachusetts Family Institute and vehement opponent of same-sex marriage, walked up and down the hallways, occasionally stopping to speak to a reporter.

Someone once told me that the key to succeeding in the political arena was to refrain from turning your adversaries into your enemies. This sounded like good advice at the time, but there was no way I could follow it now. Any recognition of gay couples was an anathema to Crews. This man was an enemy, pure and simple. And even though I knew that I saw him as evil as he saw me, at that moment I couldn't escape my purely emotional reaction. I would have joined right in if the crowd had jeered him, humiliated him, instead of singing. I would have followed the crowd without thinking, something I taught my students never to do.

I didn't want to feel this way. I wanted to rise above my visceral response and just disagree, honestly and civilly, but I couldn't find it in me. This did not make me proud.

By the end of the day, the Convention was still gridlocked, and the assembly recessed yet again until March 29th, a little over two weeks away. We'd avoided another grenade, and gay marriage was still legal. But the emotional toll of the past weeks had left me with little energy.

In class we were studying 20th-Century American history through the lens of immigration and migration. All four eighth grade teachers had agreed that we should teach about the migration of gay men following World War II. The war was the first time many gay men had met other men who shared their sexual desires. When some of these men returned home via New York and San Francisco, they could not face life back in the closet, nor could they face telling their families the truth about who they were. So many stayed in these ports, never even calling their families to let them know where they were.

We decided to show the movie *Coming Out Under Fire*, a documentary about gay men and lesbians who served in World War II. Made during the "don't ask, don't tell" debate early in the Clinton presidency, the movie is a deeply moving series of interviews with gay men and women who tried to reconcile their sexuality with their deep desire to serve their country. Some of the interviews are sexually frank ("blow job" is mentioned a few times) and I was nervous about my class' reaction, even though I knew every single student was mature enough to handle such language and every single parent would be supportive of showing the film. My colleagues had no qualms at all. One even included a brief documentary scene in which a line of naked men line up for their military physicals. In the end, I backed down, carefully fast-forwarding over these scenes to avoid my own uneasiness. The kids knew what I was doing; they didn't buy the lame excuse about wanting to get as much of the movie in as possible before the end of the day. I wondered if I had done more harm than good. I had lied to the kids – something I hadn't done since my in-the-closet days – and at the same time might have given them the message that there was something wrong about parts of the film I had skipped.

When I told Bruce about what I'd done in class, he looked at me and said, "Ken, when are you going to give yourself a break?"

"I know I should but –"

"I'm serious. You don't have to change the world all by yourself. Those kids are so lucky to have you. Don't do this to yourself."

"I'll try," I said.

"That's the point," he said. "You don't have to try. Just being who you are, just being *out*, is changing kids' lives."

I wanted to believe he was right. After all, isn't that what Shawn, my former student who'd written the article for *Bay Windows*, had said?

If I had only had one gay teacher my life would have been so much easier.

"Thanks," I said to Bruce.

"Maybe you need a break from all this," he said. "Maybe you just need to step back for a while. It'll drive you crazy if you don't."

I took my first step back when the Convention reconvened on

March 29th. At the State House, the crowd was huge, the energy overwhelming. After two hours, I was tired of standing, tired of being so physically close to so many people. I spoke for a while with a Shady Hill father who, along with his partner, had a child in the third grade whom he was now trying to entertain.

"Are you going to try to get inside the Chamber?" he asked. "After all this, we should at least be there if a vote comes."

"I think I'm going home," I said. "This is really getting too much."

I took the subway and bus back to Shady Hill where I picked up my car and drove home. I didn't even listen to the radio for updates. I didn't have it in me anymore. When I entered the house, I turned on NECN, which was providing gavel-to-gavel coverage. The vote had just been taken while I was in the car. The numbers were on the screen.

We had lost the first battle. 105 legislators had voted in support of the amendment to ban gay marriage and create civil unions. 92 had opposed it. Many of those who opposed the amendment were not gay-marriage supporters; they opposed both marriage and civil unions, and did not want to see either become law.

I sat on the sofa for a while without moving. I'd believed that we were going to lose, but believing is not knowing, and my knowing, this absolute certainty, felt worse than I'd expected.

CHAPTER ELEVEN

READY TO WED

Immediately after the vote, Mitt Romney announced that he would ask the SJC for a stay of its ruling until November 2007 when, if the legislature passed the amendment again the following year, the question would go before the voters. He enjoined Attorney General Tom Reilly to support him, but Reilly, who had publicly criticized the original SJC ruling in favor of gay marriage, refused, saying that "whether we like the decision or not, we take an oath to uphold the law." Romney therefore submitted "emergency legislation" in order to block the first gay couples from marrying on May 17th. That attempt failed as well.

Instead of wanting to celebrate – at least for now, it looked like gay marriages would happen – I remained tense. I didn't trust the political system or the power of the Catholic Church in Massachusetts, and I found myself approaching each day with the dread that some procedural maneuver no one had ever considered might out of nowhere put an end to our marriage possibilities.

I saw my therapist more than usual during this time. When I first began therapy, I went every week, but the last few years I'd been able to cope on an as-needed basis. It was clear to me that I needed to see Dr. Blakely regularly again. Bruce and I had been together for nine years, yet

I'd begun to base the future of our relationship on whether or not we'd be able to marry. *If we can't marry, then we might not last,* went the thought bubble. I knew I was giving the government far too much power over our relationship, but I couldn't help it. If marriage was so important to me, wouldn't it stand to reason that if we *couldn't* get married, we would somehow be left *less than?* I wanted the exchange of rings on our living room sofa to be enough.

My therapist and I came up with the idea to suggest to Bruce that we marry on May 17th, just in case the right was snatched away from us before our planned wedding on January 15th. We could always marry in private, then celebrate later. Bruce agreed that getting our license at Waltham City Hall on May 17th would at least give us some sense of security during the next few weeks.

Still, because we had harbored doubts about gay marriage becoming a reality, we hadn't yet told Bruce's daughters Kate and Charlotte, of our plans to wed. We'd always tried to protect the girls as much as possible from the challenges of having a gay father and "stepfather." It seemed wise to wait until we were absolutely sure the wedding would take place. We didn't tell their mother, either; while Beth had been supportive over the years and supported gay marriage, we didn't know how she'd react to our own marriage intentions. I felt like a mother in the first weeks of pregnancy: I wanted to make sure there was no chance of miscarriage before announcing our plans.

Until now, the complicated web of our relationship with Beth and the girls had worked because Beth, Bruce, and I had made it so. Bruce wanted the girls to experience parents who got along with each other. I wanted to get to know the girls, to be with them. And Beth and I genuinely liked each other; I sometimes shared a meal with her and the girls even when Bruce was away on business.

So we tried to be a normal family. We had Sunday dinners together. We attended Kate's violin recitals together. We sat together on Christmas Eve to see the girls in the Christmas pageant at their church. We even traveled together to New Orleans, booking adjoining rooms in a hotel in the French Quarter, one for Bruce and me, the other for Beth and the girls.

We'd had fun there, so Bruce proposed a trip to Puerto Rico the following year during April break, a few weeks after the legislature gave initial approval to the Constitutional Amendment banning same-sex marriage. We stayed in a hotel in San Juan's old neighborhood, Beth and the girls adjacent to us once more. We spent all of our time together except late at night when Bruce and I tried our luck on the slot machines in one of the many casinos in the city. The highlight of those first days was when we had a leisurely meal at a small restaurant run by a woman who had emigrated from Mexico. I practiced my Spanish with her. I thought I was quite rusty until she said to Bruce and Beth on our way out, "Your son speaks beautiful Spanish. He should move to Puerto Rico. He could get a great job and marry a nice Puerto Rican girl."

We use our own understanding of the world to make sense of what's in front of us. Our experience is all we have. My being Bruce and Beth's son – and Kate and Charlotte's brother – was the only way this woman could explain who we were.

The second leg of trip presented the first real challenge for us as a family. Perhaps we were naive to think that we could all live under the same roof in a villa we rented. Perhaps we should have realized that three days of tourist activities in San Juan were different from three days of leisure. Whatever the case, something was amiss. Suddenly, with nothing but time on our hands, and in close quarters, cracks began to show. We read subtexts where none were implied, felt tension where there was merely silence. I dove into reading, devouring an Anne Tyler novel on the beach in nearly one sitting. One morning Beth awoke and tried to rally us for a trip to view one of the world's largest telescopes. Bruce and the girls went along; I decided to stay back. I'm a loner at heart, and needed time and space for myself.

I think now that my own uneasiness was about Beth and the kids not knowing that Bruce and I had planned to marry. I'd grown up with too many secrets in my family. I understood the emotional toll that silence took on me as a gay man. Even as I agreed with Bruce that it was best to wait to reveal our plans, I resented returning to the closet. I'd worked hard in therapy to cultivate more honest relationships in my life. Suddenly my relationship with this extended family – especially the two girls – was drifting into new territory. I worried about what the girls would think once they finally found out about our getting married. Why hadn't we told them earlier? I'd always approached the girls with respect and integrity. Not telling them of our plans seemed to reveal a lack in both areas.

I wondered why the girls never asked us if we planned to marry. I worried that our relationship had become off limits. If you don't talk about it, it isn't there. Maybe that was how our family had survived all these years. Maybe Bruce and my relationships had become the elephant in the room.

Bruce's anxiety in Puerto Rico had everything to do with the pressures of executing the perfect vacation he had been planning for month. He'd once told me that his mother, who ran the household with an iron fist, began preparing for Christmas months in advance. She'd pick a Christmas theme and color, then decorate everything according to her rigid notion of what the holidays should look like. When she finished, she realized that even a *Better Homes and Garden* Christmas couldn't mask the sadness in her life, she grew despondent. As far as I knew, Bruce was essentially happy with his life, but he'd inherited this instinct for unrealistic expectations from his mother. Like his mother's Christmases, the flawless trip to Puerto Rico he'd imagined was impossible to pull off.

But Bruce and I did have some wonderful moments together that week. One night, we snuck out for a walk on the abandoned beach. We climbed onto one of the many large wooden beach chairs, thickly padded and surrounded by mosquito netting. He put his arm around me. The moon, the waves, the brush of a gentle breeze against our skin. I couldn't imagine a more perfectly romantic moment together.

"This is nice," Bruce said, an understatement. But it was, among many other things, simply *nice*. Normal. Somewhere else right then there was a man and a woman hugging on a beach, feeling what we were feeling. No more, no less.

I realized that no matter how hard we tried to integrate the girls and their mother into the circle of our relationship, no matter how hard we tried to create a family, the relationship was, at its core, between Bruce and me. It's a simple concept, I know, one that I'm sure most married people understand instinctively about family life. Love starts with the couple and branches out to the children, friends, relatives; but then it circles back. I don't think I understood this before our trip to Puerto Rico. I hadn't realized how we needed to reclaim our relationship as essentially *ours*. The love Bruce and I shared could never keep everyone happy. It began and ended with the two of us.

When Bruce and I had decided to go to City Hall on May 17th, I had assumed that we would privately get married that day, then hold a public ceremony on January 15th. When we returned from Puerto Rico, I discovered that this was not Bruce's understanding.

"Now, make sure you're not traveling to Texas on May 17th," I said to him one day, half-jokingly.

Bruce paused before he answer. "Sure," he said. "You're right. It would be nice if we went to City Hall together."

"It would be more than nice," I said. "Don't you think it's rather essential?"

"I don't think they require the two of us go to pick up the license. But I want the two of us to go. It's too special a day for one of us to do it alone."

"But we're doing more than pick up the license, aren't we?"

It soon became clear that Bruce had thought that we would not actually get married in May, but that we would get the license, fill it in at home, then have it ready to submit to the town clerk *just in case* it looked like the right to marry might be withdrawn between May 17th and our official wedding date.

We had different wedding dates in mind. We didn't even have the right year. I took this as a bad sign.

"But what does it matter if we get married in May or in January?" I asked. "Can't we just do the legal stuff in May and have the reception in January?"

Bruce said he'd never heard of such a thing; I reminded him that most people had never heard of two men getting married. These were unusual circumstances.

Every once in a while over the past years, the differences in our social and economic backgrounds had clashed, but never had these two worlds collided as they did that day. Bruce could not get his mind around separating the civil service and the church ceremony by eight months; I couldn't understand why we had to play by the rules of social etiquette. When I then suggested we get married on May 17th and then have a reception with twenty or so people back at the house, his face dropped.

I realized then that Bruce was hoping to have the perfect wedding, just as his mother wanted the perfect Christmas. I wondered if he'd set the bar as high for our married life, and I began to worry I'd never be able to give him that perfection. It seemed to me that one of the benefits of a nine-year engagement was that neither of us would be entering our marriage with any illusions. Or at least that's what I had hoped was a benefit.

I decided not to suggest to Bruce that our misunderstanding about what day we would be married was an ominous sign. I've learned from Bruce – or at least I've tried to learn from him – that not every mistake is heaped with Freudian significance. So I tried to approach the issue as reasonably as I knew he would. We came to an agreement that we would go to City Hall, get the license and hold onto it. If it looked like the right to marry was to be taken away from us before January 15th, we would call our minister who was also a Justice of the Peace. She and her husband lived around the corner from us. She would marry us immediately and we would beat the system.

But that plan didn't work out, either. We learned that the blood test required for obtaining a license was only good for two months, which would mean, in order to be fully prepared, that we'd have to take regular blood tests until mid-December. This did not seem like a reasonable option. We also learned that we couldn't just ask for a blank license and keep it at home. And once the request was made, the license was only good for a month. What had seemed like a reasonable plan had turned into a logistical nightmare.

So we agreed on Plan C. We would proceed as if we were having a medium-sized wedding (we didn't go into exactly what that meant) and

look for a hall, begin to think about caterers and music. If within five or six months we decided to go with the service in our living room with twenty or so guests,
we could always cancel these arrangements. Plan C kept our options open, even if we were left to hope that if the government took away our right to marry, we'd at least have a few days warning so that we could wed in time.

We decided to visit the Paine Estate in Waltham, which was less than a mile from our house. One afternoon we met Angie, who was responsible for renting the building to the public. In her cigarette-laced voice, she explained to us that along with Frank Lloyd Wright's Robie House in Chicago, Stonehurst, as the building was called, was considered one of the most architecturally significant houses in the United States. The house, which could hold at least two hundred guests, was surrounded by over one hundred acres of land. A wide curving staircase opened up onto the banquet room like a set from *Sunset Boulevard*. We loved the lodge-like feel to the place: the dark wood, the thick beams, and, most of all, the enormous fireplace that I immediately imagined roaring as we entered the house after the service. I was beginning to think I might be able to handle a "medium-sized" wedding after all.

After our tour, Angie sat us down in her office to talk details. The house was surprisingly inexpensive to rent for Waltham residents, and since January was off-season, the price would be even lower than usual. Angie told us that she had to agree to any caterer that we hired. She'd had some problems in the past, she said in a tone that implied that she was a "one strike and you're out" sort of gal. She started flipping through her sizable Rolodex, ready to provide recommendations of caterers she liked. She stopped every once in a while to jot down the telephone number of a caterer who "wouldn't have any problems with you guys."

I wasn't sure how to respond. I didn't want to deal with a caterer who'd make planning our wedding any more difficult because we were gay, so I was glad to have the information. But I was annoyed at the nonchalant way Angie approached this bigotry, as if this were something we had to handle without any feelings whatsoever. I wondered how often we'd have to come up against overt disapproval of our wedding when hiring caterers, musicians, the photographer, the florist, or the police officer required in the rental agreement.

I decided to say nothing, but take Angie at her word. She gave us the names of five caterers, then penciled us in for January 15th, 2005. We wouldn't get an official contract until November or so, but there was no need to worry: January 15th was ours. She suggested we book the caterer this summer. If it would be helpful, we could call her in August and she'd provide a list of musicians who might be interested in providing music at our reception. I wondered how we'd go about finding out if they'd object to playing the first dance for two married men.

The evening of May 16th, hundreds of gay couples lined up in front of the Cambridge City Hall to obtain marriage licenses at midnight, the earliest possible time any municipality was allowed to issue them. Bruce and I watched on TV as couples filed through the City Hall doors. It looked like New Year's Eve: all cheering and celebration. When the couples exited the building, many hugging and crying, the crowd of about 10,000 cheered. The roar silenced the voices of the handful of protesters, whose anticipated disruption never materialized, leaving the police in riot gear milling about the crowd.

The couples had not yet officially wed. By law, you had to wait three days from obtaining the license until marrying. To marry any more quickly, a special waiver was required from the court; many of these couples were planning to line up at the nearest court the very next morning, obtain a waiver, and marry on May 17th.

I held Bruce's hand as we watched. We fought back tears. What I didn't feel that night was an urge to be there with the other gay couples. As odd as it may seem for a memoirist to claim himself a private person, I would have hated being in the limelight. I still yearned for a small ceremony in the dead of winter, fire burning in the fireplace, receiving congratulations from our closest friends.

When I opened the *Boston Globe* the next morning, the headlines were enormous: *FREE TO MARRY.* I read the stories from start to finish, studied the photos over and over again, watched replays of the scene at Cambridge City Hall on Eye Opener News. I didn't know how I would make it through the day without tearing up.

The most moving moment came as I was driving to school. I decided to pass as many city halls as I could, to see if any gay couples were waiting for the doors to open. Right down the street at Waltham City Hall, a middle-aged lesbian couple stood patiently on the steps, one woman reading a newspaper as if she were waiting for a train. A few miles down the road I approached the Watertown Town Hall. It is this image that is forever etched in my mind:

Two women were sitting closely together on the steps, holding hands, watching the cars go by. With their white hair and thick shoes, I assumed they must have been in their seventies. I tried to imagine what they must have been feeling. They might have been together twenty, thirty, maybe even forty or more years. And they could now marry. After decades they could finally make it official.

I sat in my car, dazed, until a horn blared from behind.

Why were these two elderly lovers feared? How did their saying "I do" inside City Hall ruin the institution of marriage? How could anyone oppose a change in our society that made people so profoundly happy? I wanted to bring every last state senator and representative to these steps and say, "Please explain the danger here. I just don't get it."

At school, the mood was celebratory. A woman I never even knew supported gay marriage – in fact, I had assumed the opposite – hugged me in the front hall of the office building. She couldn't stop laughing. "Isn't this just an amazing day?" she said. The mood was similar in the faculty room, where a number of people came up to me and expressed how excited they were, congratulating me directly as if I were getting married that very morning. I was very happy, of course, but I couldn't get the picture of the two women on the steps of the Watertown City Hall out of my mind. It was a bittersweet image: years of being denied the right to marry were behind them, but who knew for how long they would be allowed to stay married? Who knew what the legislature would do the following year, what the voters would then do, and whether or not their marriage would be annulled? I so wanted to feel nothing but elation that morning, but the past and future of those two women pulled on me. I could only invest so far in their present.

When I mentioned to one of my colleagues what I had seen and the effect it had on me, she said, "Look, I know this may not last forever, but just for now, I'm going to let myself feel nothing but happiness at what is happening today." I wanted to write those words on my hand to remind myself that today *was* a day of pure happiness. It then occurred to me that this woman, no matter how supportive she was of gay marriage, didn't have the investment in the issue that I had, just as I would never be as personally connected to the abortion issue as a woman would be. I wondered if other gay people were feeling the way I was.

Bruce was on his way to Texas that morning, but I caught him before he left for the airport. He agreed with me that it was perfectly normal to be plagued by reservations and fears, no matter how joyous the day. We shouldn't trust the government at all, he said, explaining that he had just heard that Governor Romney and our Attorney General were ready to enforce a law from the early 1900's that prohibited out-of-state couples from marrying in Massachusetts. It didn't matter that the law had its roots in the segregationist laws of the past: its original intent was to prohibit interracial couples from marrying in the more liberal Massachusetts and returning home to states where such marriages were illegal. The law was on the books, and he could use it to keep gay marriage confined to one state.

What made enforcement of the law – ignored for many decades now – so ironic was that today, May 17, 2005, was the fiftieth anniversary of the *Brown v. Board of Education* decision which ended legal segregation in the United States. I knew that the gay marriage decision, while extremely important, would never have the far-reaching effect that Brown did. First of all, the ruling did not come from the U.S. Supreme Court but a Massachusetts SJC. And the ruling itself was fairly narrow. Once gay marriage became the law of the country, this decision could well be a blip on the judicial screen. Years from now, grandparents might have to explain to their children that there was a time when two men *couldn't* get married. Brown's effects, on the other hand, had dismantled almost two centuries of institutionalized racism. In fact, one of Brown's basic points

– that separate but equal could never be equal – had become a mantra for same-sex marriage supporters.

The evening news was full of stories, both personal and political. I'd heard enough of the doomsday predictions of what this day would do to our society, so I focused on the stories of couples who had been together for years and years, finally able to make their relationship legal. I watched Rev. Kim K. Crawford Harvie, the Unitarian Universalist minister at Boston's Arlington Street Church, marry two men who seemed both overjoyed and relieved that they could exchange vows. This was the church Bruce and I retreated to when Matthew Sheppard, the gay college student from Wyoming, was murdered in a horrific hate crime that gripped the nation. It was here that we had spent many Christmas Eves with Ed, listening to the Boston Gay Men's Chorus sing "Silent Night," the sanctuary lit only by the candles we all held.

I debriefed Bruce when he called later in the evening, then went to bed. I had a hard time sleeping. I kept thinking about the elderly couple I'd seen on the steps of the Watertown City Hall. The writer in me had begun to spin the story of their lives, much as I had done years ago when Ed and I found a postcard in a used bookstore in Maine. It was postmarked 1942 and read:

> Bob-
> If you were with me everything would be all right.
>
> Stanley

Fifteen years later, I still speculate about the relationship between Bob and Stanley. I wonder if either is still alive, if they're finally with each other, if everything ended up being all right. I just can't forget them.

And I doubted I'd ever forget the two white-haired ladies and their love story as they sat on the steps of City Hall.

CHAPTER TWELVE

FAITH RESTORED

The excitement over May 17th and the days that followed abated as my first year back in the classroom was winding down. I welcomed the distraction of Shady Hill's year-end rituals: May Day (held in mid-May instead of May 1st), yearbooks, ice cream socials, graduation night, the alumni breakfast. The last morning of the school year, I was surprised to find all the parents of my students in the classroom when I arrived. It was traditional to have a class breakfast at the end of the year, but I didn't expect so many parents to attend. The mood was both celebratory and nostalgic. I mingled about the crowd more confidently than I usually approach such gatherings. I loved these kids and their parents. I don't think they completely understood how they'd been a lifeline for me when I had seen so much hostility and hatred throughout the year.

Our parent representative asked for everyone's attention. Carol was one of my favorite people at Shady Hill. I loved everything about her: her humor, her kindness, her calm. I even loved the funky way she dressed, how she so fashionably sported her pair of laceless Converse sneakers with a skirt. She and her husband had been among the most supportive parents that year. Once Carol had quieted everyone down, Leila raised her hand and asked to speak. Leila had struggled throughout the year, but by spring had grown in confidence, especially as a writer.

"In September, Mr. Harvey sat us down and asked us what we wanted to say about ourselves as a class," she began. "We put all the words up there on the board." She pointed to a large yellow sheet of poster board with the words "our class" circled in the center. Around this circle were the qualities the kids had chosen to describe the class they wanted to have by June: *proud, confident, fun, trusting, leaders, writers, kind, supportive, ready to leave Shady Hill.* Leila's voice broke as she continued. "I think we've accomplished all these things. Thank you Mr. Harvey."

There was a collective sigh and applause.

"I've been at Shady Hill for a long time and I've always tried to do well," she went on. "But I always tried to please the teacher. Mr. Harvey was the first teacher who made me want to do well for me, for myself."

"That says it all," whispered a parent in my ear.

Leila had summed up exactly what I would have put on my poster board if someone had asked me to write down what I wanted to accomplish as a teacher. I've always felt that there is an invisibility to the good teaching; kids *should* be working for themselves, not the adults who are urging them on. It's the only way they'll become truly confident learners.

After another round of applause, Carol quieted the crowd again. She then looked at me, running her fingers along a scrapbook. She told me that all the kids in the class had written me a letter that reflected on how important the year was to them. I swallowed hard, trying not to appear too emotional. I had been an administrator and a Spanish teacher for more than twenty years. I was not used to this type of a connection with kids and families. When Carol handed me the book, I could only say thank you; I wasn't prepared to say anything else.

"There's one more thing," Carol said. I hadn't realized she was also holding an envelope. Perhaps the parents had bought a gift certificate to a bookstore in Harvard Square. Anyone who knew me knew that this would be the best gift anyone could ever give me.

"This has been a very big year," Carol said. "And I know it's been especially important for Ken and his partner. As you know, this was the year that gay people were allowed to marry in Massachusetts. To celebrate this occasion, and to help make sure that the right for everyone to marry continues, we have made a donation to Mass Equality, an organization that is fighting for the rights of gay and lesbian people to marry. We have made the donation in your name, Ken."

I was stunned. I don't think I'd ever been so moved by a gift. I knew that such an act of generosity and support could only have happened in a handful of schools in this country, if it could have happened anywhere else at all. I also knew I needed to say something in response to this gesture. My hands shaking, I stepped next to Carol to accept the envelope.

"Thank you so much," I said. "I am so deeply moved. I am very lucky. I need to tell the kids in my class that there wasn't a morning that I didn't look forward to being here with you. Driving to work, I couldn't imagine wanting to go anywhere else to spend my day. Thank you for that." I paused, trying to put together a few coherent sentences about the envelope I now held. "You're right, Carol. It *has* been a big year. But it's also been a very difficult one. I've spent a lot of time in the company of people who would do anything to keep loving couples from staying together. I've seen signs and heard words that were hurtful and mean. There were times when I lost faith in the kindness of people. But I need to tell you that whenever I'd walk into class, my faith was restored. I would sit down for morning meeting with these kids and relax. I regained my faith. I knew the world was going to be all right."

A few parents and kids had begun to cry. Perhaps it was the New Englander in me, but I couldn't let myself show such emotion in front of everyone. I thanked the class again, then walked to my desk, my back to the parents and kids I'd spent the last year with, and wiped my eyes.

CHAPTER THIRTEEN

HOUSE AND HOME

Bruce and I bought our house in Waltham in December, 2000. I was sitting on a box of books in the sun room as the burly movers carried our refrigerator down the narrow stairway from the kitchen to the cellar. One of the men lost his grip, and began shouting at the other to hold the refrigerator tight. What followed were screams and threats: *I'll fucking kill you. Shut the fuck up. I'll drop this fucking refrigerator on you, you son of a bitch.*

I sat paralyzed on the box until Bruce came in from the car. He saw that something was wrong with me, and immediately put his arm around me and asked me if I was all right.

"I've got to get out of here," I said. I explained to him that I was having a flashback to one of the violent family episodes my sister had described to me. In my mind I saw my parents. I saw myself sitting on the top step of the stairway that led from our kitchen to the cellar. I was watching my father hit my mother. I could hear my little sister yell *bitch* at him. I remembered that she was only about five years old.

Cellar. Stairs. Kitchen. *Bitch. Son of a bitch.*

I'll fucking kill you.

Bruce offered to go with me, but I told him he needed to stay and supervise the moving. I pulled out of the driveway and headed down

Trapelo Road. I had no idea where I was going; I just needed to be moving. I couldn't find the strength to sit and be with my feelings right then. I turned on the radio, looking for a piece of music, the news, an interview – *anything* – to distract me. I drove past the town library, through Harvard Square, along the Charles River. I drove down streets I'd never known existed, hoping to get lost. On one of these streets I finally pulled over. I breathed deeply.

My flashback shouldn't have been entirely unexpected, but it was. For months now I had been talking with my therapist about my anxiety about buying a house. There was no question I wanted to share a home with Bruce. But as we neared our closing date, then our moving date, I had become more and more frightened. I had no idea why. This was what I had wanted for so long.

My therapist asked me to tell him what it meant to me.

Not the Dick and Jane worlds of my literary childhood, that's for sure.

That's what it doesn't mean. Tell me what it does mean.

Drinking.

Depression.

Violence.

Fear.

And then one of us said, I don't remember who: *"You have to convince yourself that this home isn't that home."*

If Bruce was experiencing similar feelings, he didn't let on. Perhaps he had already grappled with the meaning of these words when he had married fifteen years earlier. His marriage with Beth might not have been perfect, but it certainly wasn't violent and, especially once Kate and Charlotte were born, many of his memories of house and home were happy ones.

When I returned to the apartment, the furniture and boxes were loaded onto the moving van. I went upstairs and looked around one last time. Here was the first home we'd shared together, where we had exchanged rings, where we had grown close to the elderly landlady who even tried to boy watch with me on the front porch, remarking on some of the good-looking guys in the neighborhood, then asking me if I agreed with her.

Bruce and I drove ahead of the moving van to Waltham, a ten-minute ride. I had calmed down some, but my heart was still racing. I found my bottle of tranquilizers in my backpack and took one. Bruce comforted me with his hand on my knee.

"Those guys seemed really scary," he said. "Even without the flash-back, I'd have understood it if you'd had an anxiety attack."

He was right: these were not men to mess with. Huge biceps, tat-toos, each looking like a linebacker. They had intimidated me. They made some mocking references to the number of books we had, as if they were lowering themselves to move a couple of nerdy queers. Even after they had moved us in, when they suddenly asked for a thousand dollars more than we'd agreed to, because the job was harder than they'd anticipated, we readily agreed to give it to them. "Look, Ken, they know our address," Bruce whispered to me. "Let's not take any chances."

Two days after moving in, on Ed's birthday, we bought our bas-sets, Shakespeare and Oscar; one week after that, we hosted Christmas for eight: the girls and Beth, her cousin Sue and Sue's boyfriend, Ed, and the two of us. We were crazy to think that we could possibly pull off a Christmas dinner so soon after moving in. We were equally crazy to think that two eight-week-old puppies could be easily trained amidst the chaos of our unpacking. But we did it. We ate in the den on a makeshift table of planks on saw horses. We bought a tree on Christmas Eve and decorated it on Christmas morning. Because we hadn't unpacked our music, I bought a $5.99 CD of Christmas hits at CVS that we played night and day.

We sat down for Christmas dinner. The CVS CD played. The dogs ran under our chairs. Kate sneaked her new Gameboy to the table and played with it under the tablecloth when no one was looking. Char-lotte demanded ketchup for her turkey. Beth tried quiet everyone down to say grace.

"I hardly ever get a meal like this," Ed said.

"I think I overcooked the turkey," Bruce whispered to me. "It's really dry."

"This isn't your mother's Christmas," I said. "It doesn't have to be perfect, you know."

Oscar peed on the floor.

Shakespeare jumped on Kate's lap and grabbed a piece of bread.

House and home were redefined.

I still felt frightened in our home at times. I grew anxious when, in the course of a month, we'd woken up to a series of flat tires – four in all – whenever we parked our car on the street instead of the garage. About five rear view mirrors were smashed off our cars. I assumed teenagers driving by had noticed our gay rights bumper stickers and pulled the pranks, since we'd been genuinely welcomed by our neighbors, including two lesbian couples, across the street and next door.

One day Bruce was working in the front yard when two teenage girls walked by, one of them calling him a fag. Boy, word sure got around.

But I was happy in our house and home.

I should have realized that the word *marriage* needed as much a redefinition for me, but I didn't, and I was surprised when I found myself facing some of the same anxieties over our wedding almost five years later. The marriage I'd witnessed growing up was not the marriage I wanted for myself. I never saw my father touch my mother, at least affectionately, and by the time I was in fifth grade, my mother had assumed her position on the living room couch, where she slept until my father died. I never questioned the arrangement at the time; it seemed normal to me. I remember being shocked when one of my friends told me that he'd walked in on his parents having sex one night. I tried to convince him that he must have misinterpreted what he'd seen.

After school ended in June, Bruce and I began to talk in more detail about wedding plans. I didn't reveal my fears to him since I knew they had nothing to do with marrying *him*. There was no question I wanted to spend the rest of my life with him. But my doubts started to surface as classic psychological projection. Every few days I'd ask him, "Are you sure you want to marry me?" to which he'd immediately respond, "Of course I do." I'd joke about what it might be like thirty years from now, referring to an expanding waistline, arthritis, or even mild dementia. "You ready for this?" I'd ask. I'd ask him if he really wanted to die at the fictitious gay retirement home we'd created, Lambda Acres.

Bruce, too, had anxieties about marriage even though he wanted to spend the rest of his life with me as much as I with him. One Saturday in July we met with a caterer in Newton. We'd found the caterer on our own, ignoring the list of businesses willing to work with gay couples we'd received from the events coordinator at Stonehurst in Waltham. We hadn't yet decided on the middle-sized wedding or the more intimate affair I'd desired, so we asked for estimates for a range of possibilities. We set up an appointment for tasting the foods later in the summer.

When we got home, Bruce was quiet.

"Well?" I asked. "What's wrong? Are you having doubts about all this?"

I'd been so accustomed to receiving an immediate and reassuring response to this question that the moment's pause before Bruce spoke left no doubt in my mind that he had something to tell me.

"Okay," he said. "Sit down."

He took my hand and sat me next to him on the sofa. I raced through the list of possibilities: *he's sick, he's having an affair, he's just a really good actor and doesn't love me after all.*

"Tell me," I said.

Bruce closed his eyes. I could see him rehearsing his speech, making sure he used all the right words. But why? Because he wanted to let me down easily? But from what?

"Tell me," I said again, more forcefully.

Bruce began talking about his career. I didn't hear much of what he said; I was leaping to the punch line. Was there some guy at the office he'd been screwing around with? Had he done something wrong at work and was about to get fired? Was he bored and ready to start another career? And was this a prelude to our breaking up, just as he and Beth had separated when he switched careers and went to business school?

He finally got to the heart of the matter. He explained to me that some day it was highly likely that he'd want to move out of New England. He never really liked Boston and he missed the midwest.

Well, sure, I said. We had been talking about buying an apartment in Toronto. Wasn't that why? So we could retire there some day? What was the news in this?

Bruce explained that he wanted to move before then. Maybe as soon as Kate entered college, in about three years. It would be hard for him to get a new job in Canada; both the citizenship issues and his background in American rather than Canadian business laws and regulations would hinder a career there. But Ann Arbor was a beautiful city, he tried to convince me, with a great university. It was sort of like Cambridge but without the attitude.

I was relieved at first. No lover. No illness. No illegal business dealing that would send him to some white-collar prison. But then the reality of what he was asking of me set in: he wanted me to move from this region I'd called home most of my life. From this house that had been so hard to move into in the first place. I felt I'd compromised a great deal in our relationship so that the two of us would neatly fit into the life Bruce brought with him when we met. We had decided not to have children because Bruce wondered what the effect of adoption might have on Kate and Charlotte. I'd adjusted to a travel schedule that took Bruce away from home two or three weeks a month. I'd been understanding that he needed to spend a good deal of time with Beth and the girls. And now, once his obligations were finished, he wanted to move, and wanted to uproot me with him?

If he had asked what I thought of the idea of moving, I might not have been as hurt. But the way it was stated – *There's a good chance I'll want to move from Boston in a few years* – seemed to ignore all the concessions I had made since we'd met. I had worked my life around his as much as I could. Wasn't it time for him to do likewise? Plus there was another family to consider, what about *my* family of friends, especially Ed, who both of us considered was as close to us as any blood relative.

He'd already thought of that, Bruce said. He'd like very much to invite Ed to move with us to Ann Arbor. We'd buy a house with a separate apartment for him.

We talked for a while, both of us digging in our heels. We agreed that we would both keep an open mind about moving, but I found it hard not to see the suggestion that we move as one last piece of my life I wasn't willing to give up.

"So I guess there'd be no compromise here?" I asked.

"I don't see how," Bruce said. I'd seen him this stubborn before, but about very minor issues, like the time he insisted that we request our box of popcorn at the movies only be buttered on the *left* side, so he could eat from the right and not have to deal with his lactose intolerance. But this was not the movies; this was a major life change. For the first time since Bruce proposed, I had serious doubts as to whether or not we should marry.

"Let me ask this then," I said. "Would you go to Michigan without me?"

His hesitation was crushing. Where was this man who used to joke that I was the Mary Poppins of husbands ("practically perfect in every way," to which I would respond, "What do you mean, practically?")? What had happened to him?

"I might go alone," he said. The words floated between us, a trial balloon, for a minute or so. I quietly nodded, trying to think of how to respond. Was this it? Had we reached an impasse? We'd gone years without any significant disagreement. Was it because I hadn't asserted myself? Would someone else have left Bruce over the issue of adoption? Would I now be both childless *and* husbandless?

Bruce sighed. "Of course I wouldn't go without you," he said. "I can't picture life without you. No way. What was I thinking?"

It was then that I realized that our disagreement wasn't about relocation at all. It was about Bruce trying to save a piece of himself. His life was all obligation: work, looking after his father, supporting Beth and the kids. He rarely had time to himself. He was trying to stake out a future for us in which he had options, in which every moment of every day wasn't planned. It wasn't unlike what I was going through: We were both trying to redefine marriage and home.

I also realized that Bruce's request to move had come shortly after he had moved his father's belonging on a three-day drive from southern

Florida to Pennsylvania. His father had flown to Pennsylvania a few days earlier; it was up to Bruce to pack, pile boxes in his father's car, and head north. I'd always been in awe of Bruce's willingness to care for his parents. And since his mother had died five years earlier, the demands of his father had grown. Bruce took care of all the finances, had arranged for him to move into a retirement community in his father's home town, and took a week off from work to facilitate the move from Florida. What was re-markable about Bruce was not that he willingly did these things – many children help parents in these ways – but that he did them given how little appreciation his father had shown over the years. If Bruce sometimes suffered from low self esteem, it was due in no small part to the way his father had treated him. I was only party to their relationship when his fa-ther would occasionally call and leave a message (an angry "Where the *hell* are you? I've been trying to get you all day. Call me right away and good-bye"), but Bruce had been subject to this treatment all his life. Nothing he ever did was good enough for his father. I didn't know how he continued to be in a relationship with him, let alone help him in such major ways.

Once I understood more of the reasons behind Bruce's wanting to move to Michigan – an assurance that he might finally be able to live his life, free from a world of pure obligation – I became less stubborn myself and agreed to consider the idea. I even did research about Ann Arbor on the Internet. It looked like a great place to live, but I wasn't anywhere near ready to sign on to a move. Maybe all Bruce needed was to know I would consider moving for his sake.

After I told him just that, it occurred to me that perhaps my great-est reservation about moving to Michigan was that the state wouldn't even acknowledge our marriage. It would be as if we hadn't married at all, at least in the eyes of the government. I couldn't see the point in marrying and then leaving the only state that would marry you. Why bother? We had already committed to each other when we privately exchanged rings five years ago. If we were going to move, we should head straight to To-ronto, where we could be legally married.

This raised another question for me: what did it mean to cease to be married every time we crossed the Massachusetts border? Should we bring the certificate with us, like a driver's license? If we were in New Hampshire visiting Ed and we were in a car accident, would presenting our marriage certificate make it any more likely that the receptionist at the local hospital would treat us like spouses, allowing visiting rights? I've always been one to speed down the "worst case scenario" highway. This time I didn't even slow down for the toll booths.

Bruce listened to me ramble, occasionally veering me into saner territory. I'd go crazy if I started thinking that way, he told me. We don't have control over what other states do; let's just get married for us, because it's something that we want to do, and deal with who treats us as married later.

That afternoon was the last significant conversation we had about Michigan. Bruce and I had mentioned the possibility of moving now and then, often jokingly, but it was clear that I didn't trust that the issue was completely behind us the day in July when we went to a local stationery store to order invitations. That morning, after months of presenting arguments for the wedding each of us wanted, the final decision was quite easy: Bruce announced that he understood my need for a small wedding with a reception back at the house. It sounded beautiful. It was just what he wanted, too.

That was it? Was he giving up all his leverage on the wedding and saving his compromise chips for a move to Ann Arbor? I told him that we didn't have to have the *exact* wedding I'd wanted; I'd certainly be open to some music and dancing, even an extended guest list. He would have none of it. He was serious, he said; a small wedding at the church followed by a gathering at our house with a fire in the fireplace was now his idea of bliss, too. And we could forget about Ann Arbor; this wasn't part of a larger scheme to get me to the midwest.

Much of the wedding then seemed to plan itself. We were even in immediate agreement on the wedding invitations, funky green print with a basset hound at the top. I considered it a minor victory that the woman who took our order did not look at all surprised that two gay men were marrying but rather that two gay men would have such appallingly bad taste.

When we received the proofs a few days later, we *oohed* and *aahed* over them like parents over a newborn. We even liked the small card that we would insert, requesting that guests refrain from bringing gifts but instead donate to the same gay-marriage organization that my class had chosen for the contribution in my name. What kept the invitation from being perfect was the the sole basset hound at the top. Wasn't there a way to fit two – one for Oscar and one for Shakespeare? – we asked. The woman explained why such a change was impossible, although I've since thought that the real reason was to save us from further humiliation.

"We'll get the dogs into the wedding somehow," Bruce said. "Maybe we can put the rings on little tuffets in Oscar and Shakespeare's back."

I gulped. I'd always drawn the line at dressing up the dogs in any way, even at Halloween. I refused to laugh when Bruce bought matching antlers that fit neatly over their heads on Christmas morning. I allowed only red or blue bandanas – the type that cowboys wore – rather than the kaleidoscope of colors offered at stores that specialized in gay apparel. Who knew I could be so butch?

"You're kidding, right?" I asked Bruce. "Do you expect them to walk down the aisle?"

"Of course I do."

"I'd rather move to Michigan," I said.

CHAPTER FOURTEEN

YES AND NO

Bruce and I hadn't been involved in local politics since we'd moved to Waltham. We did limited research on candidates and voted, but that was about it. The fall of 2004, however, was a different story. A local state representative who had supported gay marriage despite enormous pressure to do otherwise was now opposed in the primaries by one of Waltham's most popular politicians, a woman who had recently topped the ticket in the at-large councilor's race. She was running on the issue of gay marriage, and in this working-class, Catholic city, she was expected to be a serious opponent.

So we gave money to the incumbent, attended fund-raisers, and put a sign on our lawn. A few weeks before the primaries, the incumbent spoke at a small gathering. He was scared, he said. He thought he could lose the race. And we were scared, too. If our candidate were to be replaced by an opponent of same-sex marriage, the amendent could very well pass.

But Waltham came through. The incumbent not only won big, he carried every precinct except one. It was a huge victory for gay marriage supporters, and another sign that gay-marriage was not quite the hot-button issue to voters in Massachusetts that it was everywhere else.

The week of the primaries Bruce and I attended our first meeting with Jane Newman, our minister at the Unitarian Universalist Church where I was treasurer and Bruce had served as Director of the Annual Pledge Drive the previous year. We had started attending the church shortly after we moved to Waltham. At our first Sunday of the sanctuary, we sat in the back, tentatively singing along with the congregation, then donned our name tags and retreated for coffee hour in the church hall. We didn't find many gay people there, but what we did find was a roomful of honest, sincere people who wanted to get to know us. We were struck by how easily people approached us to ask if we wanted to join them on a ski weekend or made sure we knew they'd love to see us the following Sunday. I also realized that my upbringing in Lynn connected me with the working-class congregation.

As we entered the church for our appointment with Jane, one of two required to marry, I was anxious. I had no idea what she would ask us, what we would be required to reveal. She greeted us, gathered some binders and folders, then ushered us into a small parlor off the sanctuary. She then began our meeting by saying that she already considered us married, that what she usually did with couples at the first meeting was geared to those who had been with each other a year or two, not ten. Jane smiled as she spoke to us, seeming genuinely happy to be with us.

"What do you love about each other?" she asked.

It was a basic question, yet it took both of us awhile to answer. I didn't want to give her a mere list of Bruce's attributes, nor did I just want to gush about my feelings for him. I was relieved when Bruce decided to go first. I have always had a very difficult time accepting any sort of praise, and that evening was no different, as Bruce told Jane that I was the most ethical man he knew. I quickly ran through the litany of *un*ethical things I had done in my life, stretching far back into my childhood when I cheated on a homework assignment in the sixth grade.

He went on to talk about my talents, my kindness. He loved that I was a teacher, that I worked so well with kids, that I had developed a close relationship with Kate and Charlotte. I squirmed as he spoke; this was harder than I anticipated. I kept thinking, *what if I'm not any of these things?* Finally Bruce said, "And I think he's very handsome."

Now it was my turn. I wasn't avoiding the question when I answered that many of the qualities he loved in me were the same qualities I loved in him. I thought he was enormously kind and considerate, that he was honest, that he was good to people, that he was accepting. I then told Jane about my struggle with post-traumatic stress disorder and how Bruce had always been so patient, so willing to listen, so understanding. And I thought he was very handsome, too.

Jane listened, moved by our conversation. I wondered if she had prepared many couples who had been together so long for marriage. Would our answers have been different eight or nine years ago? Surely I had seen all these qualities in Bruce from the start. But I understood them more fully, appreciated them more deeply.

"So, what drives you crazy about each other?" Jane asked.

We laughed, but then paused. I knew I would have answered this question differently after we first met, when the bloom of love was still fresh. Absolutely nothing, I would have announced confidently. Five or six years into our relationship, I might have talked about his messiness; he would have complained about my need to keep to a predictable schedule. I might have carried on about his inability to plan while he surely would have talked about my horrible sense of direction.

I decided to speak first this time. "I really have to say that not much drives me crazy," I said. "It's not that Bruce isn't flawed. We all are, of course. But I'm not entering this marriage thinking I'm going to be swept up on a horse and live happily ever after. One of the nice things about waiting ten years before marrying is that you really *know* the person you're about to wed. This isn't all about romance. I'm marrying a real person, and I know who that person is. I've accepted the good and the bad. I try not to let things drive me crazy. What good would that do? I just try to accept. I love this very real person in my life."

Jane concluded our first session by saying that every couple has what she calls the "ritual argument." While married couples argue about many things, she felt that there was *one* issue that resurfaced over and over again, and that by recognizing what this conflict was, you could name it when it arose and move on. She thought it would be helpful if we discussed what our ritual argument was before we met with her again in a few months.

The idea of uncovering our ritual argument seemed like a very good piece of advice. When we got home, I decided that our ritual argument was, without a doubt, Bruce's inability to compromise. I had ready a list of examples of this flaw that I had tolerated for ten years. It never occurred to me that Bruce would see our ritual argument another way. He decided that our ritual argument was about where we lived. He considered himself a Midwesterner; I was a born New Englander. He saw Bostonians as cold and unfriendly; I saw them as not compromising their integrity with meaningless small talk.

"You're being way too *specific*," I said. "We don't argue about parts of the country. At least not anymore. That argument was merely a symptom of a more significant conflict in our relationship. We need to discover the art of compromise."

Bruce didn't agree. "But the whole location argument is much deeper than where we want to live. It points to how extroverted I am while you're very introverted. I'm not saying that this is a bad thing. I think we complement each other really well. But it does come up, you know, like how you hate going to parties and want to have a really small wedding."

Our ritual argument, it seemed, was deciding what our ritual argument was.

The next day, Primary Day was a highlight of the fall: Our guy won the nomination for state representative and, with little opposition, would almost certainly be elected. On that day we also began the formal process of preparing for our wedding. If only we could have felt as happy on Election Day in November

I knew all along I would vote for John Kerry, albeit with my fingers pinched tightly over my nose. He had come out in favor of the constitutional amendment in Massachusetts – the only member of the congressional delegation to do so. But at the very least, I reasoned, the ultra-conservative religious right would not infiltrate a Kerry administration. Kerry would certainly appoint more liberal leaning justices to the Supreme Court. By Election Day, I was solidly behind him. I don't know if my change of heart was a result of my increasing fear of George Bush or the sort of hostage mentality that leads one to be grateful if the captors offer the slightest humane gesture.

I voted on my way to work, arriving at the polls fifteen minutes before the 7:00 a.m. opening to a line of at least twenty-five people. I tried to convince myself that Kerry did have a chance. Maybe luck was on our side. After all, the Red Sox had just won the World Series for the first time in over eighty years.

I logged onto the Internet throughout the day, checking exit polls, noting where the heaviest voting was taking place. Late in the afternoon, one Web site had reported that exit polling was favoring Kerry in the key states of Pennsylvania, Florida and Ohio. By 6:00 p.m. the news on aol. com was asking the question, "Will Bush run again in 2008 if he loses tonight?" It was clear that the word was out that Kerry was poised to win.

Of course the exit polls were wrong. School was like a wake the next morning. Teachers were openly crying in the faculty room. Many asked me questions about our apartment (yet to be built) in Toronto and whether we were planning to move sooner rather than later. One teacher logged onto the Internet to learn the requirements for becoming a Canadian citizen. A feeling of doom seemed to touch everything that day. This was it. The United States was going to become even more fascistic and fundamentalist. It was time to be frightened. Millions of Americans had screamed "No!" to marriage equality on ballot questions across the county.

People checked in with me personally about the referendum results, expressing condolences as if someone had just died. "I can't imagine how you feel right now," one teacher said to me, which seemed to summarize what everyone was trying to convey to me. Of course I felt both defeated and outraged that eleven states had voted to write discrimination into law. But my feelings about the election went so much deeper than disappointment over gay marriage. The war. Health care. Affirmative action. The environment. Poverty. Education. There were so many other issues I cared deeply about besides gay marriage. Gay people were not the only ones who lost on that Election Day; we were only the most visible. And we were also blamed for Kerry's defeat. Newspaper columnists who dissected the election subtly but clearly put the responsibility for Kerry's loss squarely on the shoulders of those of us who defended marriage equality, rather than on the bigotry that drove people to the polls to fight it.

When I left the faculty room the morning after the election, I had yet to plan what I was going to say to my class about the results. As far as I knew, every child's family had supported Kerry; one student's mother was a lawyer for the Democratic Party who spent the day in New Hampshire observing polling sites for the type of fraud reported in 2000. We all knew how we felt about the election. The question that dogged me was whether or not it was ethical for me to express this to the class. When I had spoken to a parent about the election in early October, she said, "You know, Ken, the kids all know how you feel about the election. They just need to look at the bumper stickers on your car. Wouldn't it be better to acknowledge it? You could emphasize how you welcome different opinions, but still be honest with them."

I walked into the empty classroom and stood. It was then that I realized just how upset I was. I wasn't sure I could even bring the election up in any balanced or even-handed way. And then the idea hit me. I sat at my computer and searched for the exact wording of the Martin Luther King, Jr., quotation that had spoken to me for many years. I unrolled the white butcher paper that I kept on the shelf for art projects. With a black magic marker I wrote in thick letters: THE ARC OF THE MORAL UNIVERSE IS LONG BUT IT BENDS toward JUSTICE.

I hung the banner across the beam of my classroom, so that the kids would read it before finding their seats. I made no comment about the banner except to say that it was a favorite quote of mine and that I wished I had hung it earlier in the year. I didn't have to connect the King's words to the defeat gay marriage had taken at the polls nationally. The kids knew exactly why I had hung those words.

The next few weeks were long and I found myself getting more and more depressed. I met with my therapist, who said I was not the only patient of his who had been deeply affected by the election. I increased my dosage of one of the two antidepressants I took daily.

Our upcoming wedding did provide a respite from these dark

post-election days. Perhaps as an act of defiance, we sent the wedding invitations out the day after the election, weeks before Emily Post would have advised. But we were afraid our envelopes might get lost in the avalanche of holiday mail. We didn't include response cards but instead asked people to call us. I usually hate speaking on the phone, but as the calls started to come in, I eagerly answered. I needed some affirmation after what had happened across the country, and I got it. Call after call the response to our invitation was the same.

Yes. Yes. Yes. Yes. Yes.

The response to our invitation helped us deal with the political wounds of the November elections. What we didn't know at the time was that personal wounds – the deepest Bruce and I had ever felt since we were a couple – were on the horizon.

CHAPTER FIFTEEN

ELOPEMENT POSSIBILITIES

As Thanksgiving approached, Bruce worked on our wedding ceremony. He had briefly been a theology student at Princeton in the 1970's, and was more familiar with appropriate hymns and readings than I was. He checked in with me frequently, asking if I preferred such-and-such a passage to another. My only non-negotiable was the Mary Oliver poem I had suggested shortly after our first meeting with our minister. Bruce brought another reading to me that seemed perfect, especially since we were to be married on the birthday of Dr. Martin Luther King. It was a passage by an Episcopal priest, Carter Heyward. One line seemed especially apt for Bruce and me: "Love is a conversion to humanity – a willingness to participate with others in the healing of a broken world and broken lives." Bruce and I had both experienced these "broken lives," in part because we had grown up gay, in part because we had grown up in our particular families. Marriage was a way to help repair what had been broken. We'd already begun this process, of course, but marriage shifted our work of repairing to a permanent level. We were entering into an explicit and binding agreement that we would work to make ourselves whole as individuals and as a couple.

By early December we were right on schedule for the wedding:

the service was complete, the invitations were sent, and we'd met with our minister. The one thing we hadn't done was to tell Beth and the girls. With January 15th only a little over a month away, we couldn't wait any longer. I'm not sure what was keeping us from telling them; perhaps we were still listening to a distant voice that said this really wasn't going to happen, that we wouldn't be 100% sure of our marriage until Jane signed the certificate on the dotted line. Even then, who was to say that the legality of our marriage might not someday be called into question?

But I also know Bruce and I both hate confrontations, and although we didn't acknowledge it, I think we were both worried about Beth's reaction to our news. She'd reacted coolly when Bruce told her we'd exchanged rings a few years earlier, and for a while I found myself with my hand in my pocket in her presence so she wouldn't feel uncomfortable. Of course I should have expected her to react the way she did – wouldn't anyone in her position do the same? – but I didn't. Over the years our relationship had been so friendly that I was lulled into thinking that it existed beyond the scope of the kids and Bruce, that I wasn't just her ex-husband's spouse and a stepparent of sorts to her children. Maybe Beth did think of me independent of these other relationships, and maybe that's why the exchange of rings ended up being tricky. The rings were a reminder that Bruce had moved on, and that his primary relationship was with me. Or maybe they reminded Beth of something she wanted in her life but as of yet hadn't been able to find. Whatever the reason, I didn't want our wedding to upset the delicate balance that had become our lives.

"I'll tell Beth tonight," Bruce said late one afternoon. "I'm supposed to go out and have dinner with them, and when the kids leave the table, I'll talk to her. You want to come?"

"I think this is something between you and Beth - first and foremost," I said. "She might feel a little shell-shocked with both of us there. But call me on your cell as soon as you leave the house. Can you tell I'm anxious about this?"

"Don't be," Bruce said. "It'll work out. No worries."

No worries was Bruce's catch-all phrase for tense situations. When he was still at Beth's house at 10:30 that night, I decided I really should worry. I began to think that if Beth told Bruce our getting married was a terrible idea, he'd have second thoughts and want to cancel our wedding. The chances of this were miniscule, but by the time the 11:00 p.m. news was on, I was convinced the wedding was off.

Around 11:15 p.m. the dogs jumped onto the sofa and looked out the windows, barking their greeting to Bruce. When he came in, I knew something was terribly wrong. He barely even petted Oscar, who was begging at his feet for attention.

"Well?" I said. "Did you talk?"

"Hold on a second," Bruce said. "It's a long story. Let me get my coat off."

Shit, I thought. The conversation must have gone worse than it did in my wildest nightmares.

Bruce sat beside me on the sofa.

"Beth and I talked," he said. "But we talked a lot about Kate. It had nothing to do with the wedding."

Bruce went on to explain how late that afternoon the school had called Beth to tell her she needed to drop everything and pick up Kate at basketball practice right away. Some friends of hers had approached the guidance counselor to say that she had acknowledged being deeply depressed, and she apparently had no idea why. Kate confirmed this diagnosis when the guidance counselor removed her from class and talked to her. She was suicidal.

I was stunned. I was a teacher; it was my *job* to recognize when kids were depressed. I had referred many, many students to counseling over my twenty-five years in the classroom. I knew all the warning signs. It wasn't uncommon for kids to come to me when they were feeling depressed. How the hell did I miss what Kate was feeling? I was reminded of my father, who for many years was a dental technician, yet brought me to the dentist all of three or four times in my life. He should have known better. It should have known better.

Bruce was dealing with his own guilt, too. Kate had slipped under the radar screen in a classic way. She was the oldest child, the "hero" of the family who starred in school and athletics. We had done our best to make sure Kate wasn't under unnecessary pressure, even trying to persuade her to take a few less-challenging courses and to skip a season of sports. But she was a driven girl who, when asked in the first grade what she wanted to be when she grew up, responded, "In charge."

Bruce told me that Beth had made an appointment the very next day for Kate to have a psychological evaluation. We talked late into the night. We rehashed all the warning signs we might have missed. What had we done? What hadn't we done that we should have? Bruce and I were masters at blaming ourselves. If I thought hard enough, I'm sure I could have claimed at least some responsibility for the Iraq War.

We went to bed around two. It wasn't until after the lights were out that I realized we hadn't spoken at all about the wedding.

Bruce called me at school the next day after my second-period class.

"They're going to hospitalize her."

Without thinking, I kicked into teacher mode. I was suddenly talking to the parent of a student of mine. It was easier than speaking as the future stepfather of a suicidal teenager.

"That's good, Bruce," I said. "She'll be safe there. They'll take care of her. They'll find out what's wrong."

"Kate told the doctor she took too many sleeping pills the other night," Bruce said. "She was lucky. *We* were lucky. She didn't take enough to harm herself. She just spent the next day in a groggy state."

This didn't surprise me. I knew that psychiatric hospital beds were so scarce, that only patients in immediate danger occupied them.

"You want me to come home?" I asked. "I can get someone to cover the rest of my classes."

"I'm at the hospital right now. Can you meet me here? Kate's on the fifth floor."

"Give me about half an hour."

It was bitter cold as I ran to my car in the school parking lot. I quickly scraped some ice that had reformed on the driver's side of the windshield, leaving a jagged patch of visibility. I then turned the defroster on high as I pulled onto the street, but the air was cold, so I began wiping the inside of the windshield with my sweater sleeve even though the frost was on the outside.

I parked in the garage beside the hospital, then ran across the walkway to the lobby where a friendly woman in her seventies told me Kate's room number. I was apprehensive as I stepped onto the elevator in the hospital. My anxiety only heightened when I approached the psych ward. On the bolted doors were instructions to ring the bell and wait for an attendant, along with a caution to be aware of "elopement possibilities." I snickered. The word made the potential escape of psychiatric patients seem utterly romantic. Maybe the sign was telling me something. Maybe that's exactly what Bruce and I should explore. Would it be so bad to sneak away and wed? Bruce could claim out-of-town business obligations; I could plead a necessity to get away with him for a day or two. Yes, I thought. Elopement was not only a possibility, it was exactly what we should do.

I was relieved when a woman dressed in black pants and a sweater opened the door. I think a formal uniform would have made me want to turn around and leave. The nurse escorted me to a desk where she presented me with a sign-in sheet requesting my name, time of arrival, and relationship to patient. I didn't know what to write. My relationship with Kate didn't have a name, at least not a familial or legal one like father, stepfather, or even uncle. I would someday be her stepfather, at least in Massachusetts, but right now I had no label. I panicked. What if they wouldn't let me in if I weren't legally related to her? She had just been admitted only a few hours ago. They might restrict visiting to the immediate family for the first few days.

If nothing else, our wedding would give me a name. Kate and Charlotte would be able to call me something that would be immediately recognizable. I understood, as if for the first time, that the very absence of a word to describe my present relationship to the girls was a symptom of how society had devalued my relationship not only with their father but also with them.

I waited until the nurse was engaged in a conversation with a colleague before I scribbled the word "family" on the relationship line, hoping she would be distracted enough not to probe any further. I consulted the chart on the wall to find out where Kate's room was, then quickly snuck away from the desk before the nurse could ask questions about me.

I found Kate sitting on her bed reading a book, her head propped up against a pillow. The bed had been made so perfectly that even with Kate on top it, it could have passed the West Point test and bounced a dime. This, almost more than seeing Kate, immediately saddened me. It was as if the staff had tried to present as meticulous an image as possible to camouflage the inner turmoil that brought the patients here.

Kate looked up at me and said hello. She seemed genuinely happy to see me, even if she looked exhausted, with deep shadows under her eyes.

"Where is everyone?" I asked. "I came here for a party, and damn it, I want it." I'd always played this role with the kids, the one who was there with the quick joke, the one who made them laugh.

"They're at a meeting with the doctors," Kate said. "They should be back in a few minutes. Or at least I hope they are. I feel like the longer they meet, the longer I'll have to stay here."

"No worries," I said. "You'll be out soon."

The pause that followed wasn't necessarily awkward; it was as if we were both taking in the enormity of what had happened that morning.

Finally I said, "Did you see the sign out there? It said you have to be really careful in order to avoid the possibility of elopement. Do you plan on eloping soon?"

Kate laughed. "This place is strange. Did you see that woman who walks around talking to herself?"

"You're not there yet," I said.

She laughed again.

Okay, I thought. Enough of the vaudeville act. I needed to say something, and what I needed to say wasn't funny.

"Kate," I said. "I know this will make you feel uncomfortable, but I've got to say it. I just want you to know that there's nothing – absolutely nothing – that you could tell me about yourself that would make me love you any less."

I didn't know whether she would accept such honest emotion from me. It occurred to me that I hadn't told her I loved her very much in her life. I was always afraid of overstepping boundaries, making her feel uncomfortable. I also assumed she'd always know. Yet right then another reason for my reticence came to me: I had been like my parents when it came to expressing love to Kate and Charlotte. Perhaps my behavior was not as extreme. After all, I had told the girls I loved them at least a few times. But I had essentially avoided expressing that love. I was overwhelmed with grief at that thought, and looked down for a moment in case I started to cry.

Kate eyes began to well. She wiped her nose with the sleeve of her sweatshirt.

I took a deep breath. "There. Now that's said. Just know that it's true."

"Thanks," Kate said.

I wanted to go on. I wanted to tell her that I was about to become her stepfather, that she could count on me as much as she ever counted on Bruce and Beth, but I knew I couldn't, I just couldn't, even as I knew it was the right thing to do. Look, Ken, you're not the professional today, I told myself. You know all those hard meetings you've had with parents? You know the meetings you had in the high school where you taught in the eighties when you had to talk to parents about drug abuse and psychiatric care and the best way to deal with depressed kids? It really doesn't mean anything, at least not right now when you're so emotionally involved. Your job is to keep the boat from rocking any more than it already has. Period. So when I heard Bruce's "hello" from the door, I didn't go to him and hug him, even though I wanted to in the worst way, because I didn't want to put him in an awkward position with Beth standing right behind him. Things were tense enough.

"I'll give you guys time alone," I said.

"You don't have to leave," Bruce said.

"It's okay. I'll just sit in the waiting room."

I stepped outside the room. A young bearded priest was approaching. He extended his hand.

"I'm Kate's youth advisor," he said. "You must be Bruce."

I wondered how I should correct him. Perhaps I should just introduce myself as the family friend. My reaction to the clergy was almost Pavlovian. I immediately felt I'd be judged, even by the Episcopal priest who came from a congregation of liberal thinkers.

"I'm Ken," I said, without explanation. To my amazement, he knew who I was. He took me by the arm and said, "So you're Ken. I hope you know how important you are to Beth and the girls. They really love you."

All I could do was thank him. I sat at the far end of the common room, as far away from the blaring TV as possible. I closed my eyes and tilted my head back, took a few deep breaths.

What about the wedding?

The question came to me out of the blue, and I felt guilty for even considering it.

Kate was sick. How can you even think about the wedding now?

Maybe the mere fact that you are thinking about the wedding shows how little you've been there for Kate.

But I *was* thinking about the wedding. The invitations had been sent; responses made.

We should cancel. We should start calling people and tell them the wedding is postponed until the spring. I can hear questions the already.

"Oh, no. But why? We were so looking forward to it."

"Is there anything wrong?"

"Are you okay? Is Bruce?"

"If I were you, I'd get married as quickly as possible before the legislature or the governor…"

I rehearsed some responses.

Not enough people could make it that weekend.

Something's come up.

We've had a family crisis that we need to tend to.

We need to postpone the wedding because Bruce's daughter is suicidal.

Maybe e-mail. A letter. A phone chain.

I would suggest to Bruce that we put off the date until spring.

I pushed the wedding thoughts aside and picked up a book to bring to the psych ward for the long periods of waiting that inevitably accompanied hospital visits. Reading had always been an anchor for me, especially during difficult times. I will forever associate reading Peter Taylor's final collection of short stories with my father's death bed, a biography of Woody Allen with an especially painful breakup, *The Remains of the Day* with feeling deeply homesick while I was in Mexico one summer. Now Kate's hospitalization and Colm Tóibín's *The Master*, a fictional account of the life of Henry James, would be forever linked.

I had been reading for about ten minutes when Bruce sat down next to me.

"Thank you for coming," he said.

"Of course," I said. "You don't have to thank me." I wondered if, after we were married, being present during an emergency would simply be expected, as it would be of any family member. You don't thank your husband for showing up at the hospital when one of the kids is sick.

"They don't know how long they're going to keep her," Bruce said. "They're not sure what's going on, but one thing they do know is that she's really depressed. It runs in the family. I don't know why we should be so shocked."

He had a point. If Kate had been in the hospital for any other disease that she might have inherited, we wouldn't have been so surprised, nor would we have blamed ourselves. How could you blame yourself for a kid with diabetes?

"But she did mention a few specific things to the doctor that are hard for her," Bruce said. "She hates school. She doesn't fit in. She's tried her best, but she just can't cut it with the boy-crazy fashion queens she has to be with every day."

Bruce and I both knew what it was like not to fit in. We also knew that Kate was never like the girls in school, even as far back as first grade. She was more assertive, more physically active. She was more likely to want to spend the night in a tent outside than go to a pajama party.

"What can we do about it?" I asked.

"We're just going to try to get her through the rest of the year at Carlisle," he said. "But after that, she wants to get out. She wants to find someplace new."

For about five years in the 1990's I had been the advisor who counseled kids where to go after they left Shady Hill.

"I think I could be helpful here," I said.

"That would be great," Bruce said. "But it's not just the school. She needs to get out of Carlisle. She told the doctor she'd like to live with us. We're closer to most of the private schools anyway. And she could try Waltham High if she wanted to."

"Of course she can live with us," I said without thinking. Isn't that what a parent does? I was as happy with my gut response as I was that Kate wanted to live with Bruce and me. I really *was* her stepfather, a parent, someone responsible for her well-being.

"It wouldn't be until June," Bruce said. "She needs to finish out the year where she is. But then she'll move in."

"What about Beth? What does she think?"

"She's okay with it," he said. "She knows it's for the best."

I pictured myself waking Kate up for school, making her lunch (well, okay, giving her lunch money), checking to make sure she had finished her homework, telling her to drive carefully before she went out for the evening.

I saw myself not just as a husband. I was also going to be a parent.

CHAPTER SIXTEEN

WEDDING DAY

Bruce and I didn't speak about the wedding during the days following Kate's admission to the hospital. Nor had we mentioned Christmas – just a few days away – even though we knew that for Charlotte's sake we needed to mark the holiday. The presence of Christmas decorations in the psychiatric ward of the hospital – they'd added a few cutouts of Santa on the walls to complement the silver tree with the small red bulbs – did little to inspire holiday cheer. I couldn't imagine Kate spending Christmas Day here, but no discharge date had been set.

Kate's diagnosis of bipolar disorder a few days after she entered the hospital did help put to rest some guilt that I was somehow responsible for her depression, that my arrival when she was six years old had so disrupted the family dynamics that she'd been scarred for life. In my more lucid moments I remembered that Bruce and Beth had divorced before we'd met. I could even make the argument that I had made Kate's life better by helping provide stability. And then there were comforting words from her doctors. They told us that mood swings can manifest themselves in exercise, so it's no wonder we didn't see the symptoms. Running hardly qualifies as cause for alarm, and Kate's depressive states were just as subtle. But there were moments when I couldn't recall these words, and right-wing mantras that I'd heard all my life played in my head: *All kids deserve to live with a mother and a father. Homosexuality damages families. You're just a selfish adult who satisfied your own emotional needs at the expense of children. Marriage is a sacred bond between one man and one woman. What are you thinking of, marrying a man?*

I was lucky to have begun a friendship with another writer who was a Shady Hill parent at about that time. Joan, who was writing a memoir about her father's suicide, said something to me while we were having coffee during Kate's hospitalization that to this day has been a help. When I suggested that I had been wondering if Kate's unconventional family life had somehow contributed to her depression, her response was purely emotional, so immediate that she didn't have time to think.

"Oh, my God, Ken," she said, "you didn't go *there*, did you?"

It was the incredulousness in her voice that made me realize that it made no sense whatsoever to visit those places of guilt about my relationship with Bruce.

Then, just as quickly, Joan added, "Of course you went there. You go everywhere."

You do. I did. But I left Joan that day believing again that getting married wasn't just good for the two of us, it was absolutely the right thing to do for the kids, too.

I broached the subject with Bruce. "Do you think we should still have it?" I asked. It was the first time in a days that we'd talked about the wedding.

Bruce thought for a moment. "Yes, I think we should," he said. "It's a month away and Kate should be better by then. I do think we should reconsider –"

"Going to Toronto for the honeymoon?"

"Yes," Bruce said, nodding his head. "I'm not sure being away for three days would do any of us any good."

"Of course," I said. "That makes sense."

I agreed completely. We'd have our honeymoon sometime, maybe in Toronto, maybe somewhere else. I was even ready to postpone the wedding if Bruce felt it would be best.

We didn't agree on whether or not we should tell Kate about our impending marriage. I believed it might help Kate if she knew Bruce and I were formally acknowledging our relationship. Beth and Bruce decided it would be best to not tell her until after we had wed. I retreated, reminding myself that no matter how big a role I played in Kate's life, Beth and Bruce *were* her parents. But I also wondered if Kate would have been kept in the dark even without her health crisis. To this day I can't answer that question.

If we had put our wedding on the back burner, then Christmas wasn't even on the stove. Bruce tends to be a year-long shopper, picking up Christmas presents for people when he's on business travel throughout the country, while this year, anticipating the month of December to be filled with wedding planning, I had done a good deal of my shopping in November. However none of us – Beth, Bruce nor I – had even mentioned Christmas Day itself. The tradition was that Bruce and I would drive out to Carlisle early Christmas morning to watch the kids open their presents, then return to our house where Bruce would prepare the dinner for Beth, the girls, and Beth's cousin. Before he moved to New Hampshire, Ed would join us as well.

The year Kate was hospitalized, we didn't even mention the family meal until Christmas Eve. Kate was released from the psychiatric ward on December 23rd, which felt like celebration enough; the details of how we would spend Christmas Day with her didn't even enter our orbit. Bruce and I had driven to Ed's in New Hampshire shortly after we watched Charlotte in the annual Christmas pageant at her church. We'd given Ed his Christmas presents and received ours, visited for a while, then headed back to Waltham around nine o'clock in the evening.

"Do we have any idea what we're doing for dinner tomorrow?" I asked.

Bruce drew a blank. We'd skipped the Christmas tree this year; in our shuttling back and forth to the hospital, neither of us had the energy or the time to put one up. But I couldn't imagine canceling our family meal. It seemed more important than ever that we share some time together, so I suggested that we call for reservations at a nearby restaurant, giving everyone the day off in the kitchen. Since no one had done any food shopping at all, this seemed like the only logical course of action.

We brainstormed some restaurants that might be open on Christmas Day, from the Park Plaza Hotel in Boston to the Westin only a mile or so from our house in Waltham. Every one was booked. No openings whatsoever, even later Christmas evening. I imagined the final scene in *A Christmas Story*, when the entire family ends up eating in a Chinese restaurant because dogs have stolen the roast turkey.

We finally thought of the Marriott in Waltham, where I'd attended more than a few proms when I taught high school. Any other Christmas I'd never have wanted to go back, but when Bruce turned off his cell phone and announced that they had a table for five at 3:00 p.m., the Waltham Marriott seemed like the Ritz.

I don't remember everything Bruce and I gave each other that Christmas Eve. As usual, I'm sure that we ended the evening with piles of books beside us. One gift I do recall quite clearly was a small Inuit-designed marble bear I put in Bruce's stocking that I had bought in Canada the previous summer. We'd both always had a fondness for bears – me because the polar bear was the mascot of Bowdoin College, my alma mater, and he, well, Bruce just liked bears. I'd seen him eye these Inuit sculptures at Canada so I snuck off to buy one while he was taking a nap at the B & B.

We woke up early the next morning to make it to Carlisle for breakfast and gift opening. Beth and the girls were in their nightgowns while Bruce and I wore baseball caps to keep our hair in place since we hadn't had time to shower. I was touched when Beth and the kids presented me with an iPod, a bit extravagant, it seemed to me. But I accepted it with genuine gratitude and appreciation – not so much for the gift, but for thinking of me at all this Christmas.

I wouldn't say that there was an overwhelming sadness to the holiday that morning, but the spirit was gone, even on Charlotte's part. Who could blame her? Dinner, too, took on a subdued tone, as if we were all seeing through a gauze curtain that kept the world hazy. The family crisis may have pulled us together, but at times it also bred a strange formality among us, and we chose our words with excessive care. We'd gotten lost on the way to the restaurant, even though it was no more than ten minutes from our house, which seemed almost too appropriate, too much like a novelistic device: the five of us trying to find our way in terrain that was at once recognizable and utterly foreign. Or Bruce and I embarking on this new journey called marriage, even though we'd been partnered for ten years,

But we made it through the day, and Kate, Charlotte and their mother left the morning of the 26th for their annual visit to Georgia to visit Beth's parents, leaving Bruce and me with time to focus once again on the wedding, which was only a few weeks away.

We should have had a to-do list a mile long that we systematically checked off, but we were both exhausted and spent much of the next few days sleeping. Even I, the early riser, slept until nine or ten o'clock in the morning, three hours later than my usual time. Bruce needs a good deal more sleep than I do – upwards to nine hours a day – but under the emotional strain of the past few weeks he couldn't get enough of it. He slept late, got up for a while, then went back to nap. Concern about depression hovered over me those days; he hadn't been seeing a therapist while I was able to keep regular appointments with Dr. Blakely all during Kate's hospitalization.

"Bruce," I said one night. "Are you sure you're up to getting married right now? If you don't think it's a good time, we really should talk about it. I'll understand," I said, hoping that if he did want to postpone, I would be generous enough to support him.

Bruce thought for a moment. "No, I want to."

"Are you sorry the kids won't be coming?"

"Of course I am," he said. "I just don't think it would go over well right now. It's coming at such a hard time. But we could always get married on the 15th as planned, then bring the kids to Canada sometime and get married with them there. If we're ever going to move to Canada, we'll want to get married there as well, right?"

This made sense to me. Because the United States federal government would not recognize our marriage from Massachusetts, foreign governments would not either. Gay marriage was legal in Canada, so the solution was simple. We'd get married twice.

"Sounds good to me," I said, but I was still dealing with my lingering doubts about his desire to continue with the wedding as planned. I didn't want to push too hard, but I also didn't want to show up at the altar with a man whose heart and mind were not present.

"Last chance," I said. "If you want to postpone, tell me now."

"No," Bruce said. "Let's go for it. Absolutely."

Because we had been so focused on Kate the last few weeks, neither of us realized how much work had to be done before the wedding. We hadn't bought our suits. One room of the house was still filled nothing but paint cans and lumber. We hadn't conferred with the caterers for months. The service wasn't complete. And then there were the flowers, the wedding cake, the general housecleaning, the question of what to do with out-of-town guests. Elopement was beginning to look like quite a reasonable possibility.

We began with the house. I spent the last few days of the year sanding and staining while Bruce worked on the electrical wiring for the sconces we had bought. This required a great deal of trust on my part; I wasn't convinced he knew exactly what he was doing. Within a day or two, it was clear we would need some outside help. We called a contractor in the area to finish the bookshelf installation, hang the wallpaper, and paint the ceiling. We were told they could come the Wednesday before the wedding and that the job would take three days. *Wednesday. Thursday. Friday.* We were cutting it close, but hadn't we been cutting it close for over a year, when the SJC handed down its marriage decision with only one vote to spare?

A few days before New Year's, we drove to Filene's Basement in Newton to buy a suit for me. Bruce had decided that he'd wear one of his dark business suits, but I didn't own one, and we needed to find one and have it tailored within two weeks. We settled on a dark blue pinstripe that matched Bruce's suit, then bought two pair of matching black shoes. At the checkout line we took a business card for a local tailor whom I called immediately to inquire if the job could be done in a week. It could. I dropped Bruce off at home, then headed straight for Sergio the Tailor, who removed pin after pin from his clenched mouth to fit me. When he inserted the last pin, he brushed my pants, stepped back, and nodded, the expression on his face never changing. "Next Saturday," he said, his Italian accent thick. "The 8th. Okay."

As I drove home, the wedding was beginning to seem real.

I hadn't given much thought to what I would call Bruce after we'd married. The term "step daughters" might not seem like the most affectionate of terms — lest we forget I was not their *real* father — but at least I now had a name for my relationship with the girls. I would no longer need to call them "my partner's children," then offer an explanation as to exactly what that meant. But I had mixed feelings about Bruce's new title. I wanted to be married, to be his husband, but I had reservations about using the word publicly. If it didn't conjure up images of cowboys or businessmen, the word "partner" was perfect. I was self-conscious about the word "husband." I'd been taught that only a woman could use that term for her spouse, and forty-six years of cultural indoctrination ran deep. I wanted to *be* his husband but I wasn't sure I wanted to deal with people's reactions when I used the term.

Our New Year's celebration that year was, as usual, quiet. Neither of us had ever enjoyed spending the evening in a big crowds, at least not since we were in college. We went to the early show our local movie theater to see *Sideways*, a buddy movie about two guys who go to the wine country in California as a final fling before one of them gets married. The future groom can't resist a young woman he meets on the trip and he questions whether or not he should ever get married at all. I loved the movie even though it was about straight guys and straight marriage. And I couldn't relate at all to wanting that last fling before marrying Bruce. I was 46 years old. I was ready and I knew it.

We returned home for a dinner that Bruce had prepared, then started a fire while Bruce put the finishing touches on the ceremony. I reviewed our to-do list as well as our already-done list. I double-checked the invitation list, just to make sure we'd heard from everyone. Then I looked over the few contracts and orders we'd arranged for the wedding: the cake, the flowers for the house, the church sanctuary, the house cleaners, and, finally, the caterer. The menu looked fine, the arrival time looked fine, but my stomach did somersaults when I read the date: January 16th. We were getting married on the 15th.

"Bruce?" I said tentatively. "I think we have a problem here. As in a major problem. Did you notice the mistake on the contract when you signed up the caterer?"

"Why? What's wrong?"

When I showed him the date, he didn't seem to immediately grasp the gravity of the mistake.

"They'll be delivering the food to an empty house," I said. "We're getting married the day before, remember?"

"Shit," he said. "I'll call them first thing Monday morning."

Because our reception was small, Bruce was able to change the date, although I can only imagine what the caterer thought when one of the grooms called less than two weeks before the event to explain he'd mistaken the day of his own wedding. While there were no other significant blunders in the days leading up to January 15th, there was still a certain degree of chaos, which, I assumed, was typical of most weddings, even modest ones with a short guest list and a wine and *hors d'ouvres* reception back at the house.

I was lucky enough to be able to take a few days off from school right before the wedding since I had an apprentice teacher that year who, as part of her training, was required to spend a "solo week" in the classroom without me. I selected the wine and beer, picked up my suit from the Italian tailor, ordered a prescription of valium for Oscar and Shakespeare so they wouldn't have nervous breakdowns during the reception, renewed my prescription for valium so that I wouldn't have a nervous breakdown at the ceremony, bought small gifts for the two ushers and readers we'd asked to be part of the wedding. Bruce spent the week supervising the carpenter and wallpaper hanger who were working against the clock to finish the library. We both had a panic attack when the paper hanger announced that he didn't think we had ordered enough wallpaper for the job, but that he would do his best to try to make what we had ordered stretch. He finished the job with about one square foot left over.

The caterer had arranged for the plates, cutlery, wine glasses, trays, and bar to be delivered the afternoon before the service. The man who made the delivery was not an employee of the caterer, but of the moving company the caterer had hired. He was a big man, clearly someone used to heavy lifting. He brought up the first stack of plates and placed them in the front hall. We chatted a bit, and in the course of the conversation I made reference to marrying Bruce. The mover said nothing more, but when he returned to his truck and unloaded the rest of the supplies, he placed them by the garage door. When I asked him if he needed some help moving the crates and tables into the house he said, "These things are pretty heavy and I'm tired. I'm just going to leave them right here. You can do it." His refusal to do what he was hired to do may have been due to his being tired, I suppose, but I was skeptical. I made a mental note to notify the caterer after the wedding.

For our "honeymoon" we decided to go to an upscale Italian restaurant within walking distance of our house, so I made reservations for the following evening. Bruce's errands that afternoon included picking up the flowers for the house – a blanket of roses for the fireplace mantel and arrangements for the library and dining room. A friend from our church picked up the cake. I recorded Baroque music to play in the background at the reception. I went through the house after the housecleaners left to make sure everything was spotless.

The house, the two grooms and the two dogs seemed about as ready as they'd ever be.

I woke up earlier than Bruce on Saturday morning. I rolled over and whispered, "Today's the day. You only have a couple of hours to back out."

"Not a chance," he said. "But I would like a little more sleep."

I got up and fed the dogs. I looked at the prescription for their tranquilizers and read that I was to give one to each "an hour before action," a phrase that struck me as funny since they had been neutered at six months. How much action could they have?

I started brewing coffee and paced while I waited for it to drip. I poured myself a cup and paced while I drank it. I retrieved the newspaper from the front steps and paced as I read it. I paced. I paced. I paced.

I knew it was typical to be nervous on one's wedding day, but I couldn't articulate what I was nervous *about*. I'd grown up with a fear that I'd pay for every good event in my life with a painful one. I'd spent years in therapy trying to figure out where this fear came from. It might well have been a symptom of the PTSD and my need to always be on guard for the unexpected, to protect myself. Maybe there was some fundamentalist god with right-winged angels who kept score, that celestial Peeping Tom who, once he saw the scales tip to the side of happiness, immediately tried to balance my life with a few choice downers.

I forced myself to sit down and do the crossword puzzle in the newspaper, an attempt at normalcy that worked for about ten minutes. I returned to the bedroom to see how Bruce was doing.

Sound asleep.

I nudged him. "Honey, wake up. We're getting married today."

"Right. Right," he said as he took off the mask he wore at night for his sleep-apnea. "I knew that."

"Very funny," I said. "It's time."

The doorbell rang. A florist was delivering flowers from Ed in New Hampshire. We still weren't sure if he'd be able to make it. He'd been having heart problems for over a year now and could never know for certain if he'd have the energy to follow through on plans.

Then my sister called.

"We're all sick as dogs here," she said, going on to explain she had to take my niece to the hospital the night before because she had spiked a dangerously high fever. "I'm really sorry."

So was I. Her absence meant that neither Bruce nor I would have a relative at the wedding.

They could see the photos, if they wanted to. Then I realized that we'd never even thought about a photographer. Nor an autograph book for guests to sign as they entered the church. I wondered where the record would be of our marriage. What could we show Kate and Charlotte to share the day with them?

We'd tell them. We'd show them the service. We'd show them the marriage certificate. Wasn't that what counted most?

I was becoming increasingly anxious that I'd forgotten yet something else of even greater importance, so I decided it was time to medicate Oscar and Shakespeare. It was easy to administer the tranquilizer to Oscar; I just pretended the pill was a snack, and he came running toward me, snatching it out of my hand. Shakespeare was a trickier sell and demanded an appetizing slice of cheese wrapped around the tiny white Valium. I stood watching them for a few moments, waiting for them to calm down – I guess I mean waiting for *me* to calm down – but nothing happened. I finally removed the gate from the stairway leading to the second floor bedroom so the boys could get Bruce up, since I hadn't been successful all morning.

The caterers came while he was in the shower. They scoped the place out, then set up shop in the kitchen. I was relieved to see that they were young far more likely to feel comfortable around a gay couple. It was a ridiculous assumption – prejudices come in all ages – but it calmed me. And the catering staff *was* kind. Even if they hadn't ever catered a gay wedding, they'd surely catered a commitment ceremony or two. But I was looking for any sign that today was going to go well, and I got it from the two women in the kitchen and man who was setting up bar in our library.

By now Oscar was staggering like a drunken sailor. His hips swiveled; his neck bounced up and down like a spring-necked toy dog in the back of a '57 Chevy. Shakespeare had merely quieted down, but Oscar's eyes drooped heavily.

Bruce came down the stairs in jeans and a sweatshirt. We still had a few hours until the ceremony; there was no reason for him to be dressed to go. But when he went to the closet to get his coat, I began to wonder if he was cutting it too close.

"I don't think you have time to *go* anywhere, Honey."

"I really need a haircut."

"You *what?*"

"I'm just going to get a quick haircut," he said. "I'm looking pretty shaggy around the neck. I'll be right back. I'll just go to that cheap place down the street."

Bruce has been balding prematurely for years; he didn't need an expensive salon to touch up his hair.

"Promise me you'll be back in a half hour, tops."

"I will. I will. Don't worry."

I did worry. I decided it was time for my own tranquilizer, so I took one with a large glass of water. Meanwhile Oscar was staggering even more; Shakespeare was yawning, producing a high-pitched squeal.

I'd already done as many "last inspections" of the house as Cher had done goodbye tours, but I did yet another anyway. And behold! On this fifth and *really* final inspection, I noticed that the men who worked on the library had forgotten to cover up the hole in the ceiling where the overhead light and fan had been removed. On the attic stairs I found the small round piece of metal that was intended to cover the hole. I stood on a chair and inserted it, but wasn't sure how to attach it to the ceiling. I was standing on the chair when Bruce, freshly coiffed, returned from his cheap haircut, about fifteen minutes later than his promised time of return. I explained the problem with the ceiling to him.

"I should probably go to Home Depot to get some screws, then," he said.

I stepped off the chair. "You're getting married in a little over an hour. There's no *way* you're going to Home Depot. We'll just need to fix it with what we've got."

I'd learned many years before that Bruce was an adrenaline junkie: he loved the feeling of making it to a destination just in time. Running toward the airport gate, jumping out of a taxi in the financial district of New York City for a meeting, booking three client meetings within minutes of each other in different neighborhoods of Dallas: what bliss! But our wedding? Sorry. No way. I told him he needed to get dressed right away.

Even when we're running late, I somehow usually manage to get us to our appointments early, and our wedding day was no exception. We entered the church through the back door, forty-five minutes before the ceremony. Maureen, our friend from the church and president of the congregation, greeted us with a "What are you guys doing here? You're supposed to come a few minutes before it starts. We're here to take care of things."

We talked her into letting us stay. When she discovered that we'd forgotten to buy a guest book for signatures, Maureen sent her husband to the local party supply store.

We'd chosen as ushers two friends of mine from school. Dennis was Assistant Head of the school. We'd become good friends when I was on the administrative team as Middle School Head. John was the wood-working teacher whom I'd known for well over a decade.

"So what should I say?" John asked as Maureen pinned his bou-tonniere. "Groom's side or groom's side?"

I laughed. "We're not going with sides. Just seat people anywhere."

Bruce and I retreated to the church kitchen. We didn't say much; I continued to pace while Bruce, always the calmer of the two of us, sat quietly on a stool. I wasn't nervous about getting married. I was worried about getting married in front of a church full of people.

"When we're up there, who should I look at?" I asked Bruce. After all, he had done this before.

"Just look at the person who is talking," Bruce said. "That is, if you're not looking at me."

I smiled. Bruce never had a problem looking me straight in the eyes.

"Thanks," I said. I kissed him. "Wow. Our wedding day."

Maureen came into the kitchen to let us know that Jane, our min-ister, had just arrived. We walked to Jane's office where she stood holding three stoles: solid purple, rainbow-colored, and one that was handmade with globes and chalices.

"I always let the couple pick which one I wear," she said, holding each stole up individually.

I know the expected choice would have been the rainbow-colored stole; it almost seemed the politically responsible thing to do. But I was tired of politics. I just wanted to get married and pick the stole we wanted.

"I sort of like the handmade one," I said to Bruce.

"Me, too."

"Then this one it is," Jane said, putting the stole around her neck so that the ends fell to her knees. "It's the most popular one, you know."

We presented Jane with two books on gay marriage as a thank you for performing the service, then peeked out to see if anyone had arrived. Ed was sitting in the front row; he had made it after all. We entered the sanctuary to greet him. For a moment I felt as if I were sneaking into the audience a few moments before the play began – a professional *faux pas* of the highest order. But when I saw Ed smiling, any feeling of violating the rules of etiquette evaporated. After all, wasn't one of the rules to avoid seeing your spouse before seeing him at the altar? We'd already shattered so many rules of tradition by marrying, that stepping into the sanctuary seemed trivial in comparison.

"Wow," Ed said. "You guys look so handsome."

"Thanks," Bruce said. "We're really glad you could make it."

"I'm not coming back to the house for the reception," he said. "That would be pushing it. But I wanted to be here for the ceremony if I possibly could."

I ushered Ed to a seat at the end of the pew in case he felt ill during the ceremony and needed to leave.

"You know," he said. "I'm seventy-one years old and this is my first wedding."

"You're kidding."

"My first and last," Ed said. "I don't know anyone else who could possibly get married. I get to go to one wedding in my life and two men are getting married. It's perfect."

When I hugged Ed, I noticed Kurt, a friend of mine who had a stroke on his fortieth birthday. He'd undergone years of therapy and was able to walk with the help of a cane. It was enormously moving to see how far he'd progressed. Only a few years ago, he could never have made it to the wedding.

"I got here a little early," Kurt said. "Like two hours ago. It was the only train I could catch from Boston." Kurt lived in an assisted-living complex near Fenway Park.

"But you made it," I said, patting his hand. "Thank you."

"Here, I've got something for you," he said. "It's a combined wedding and Christmas present." He slowly reached into his coat pocket with his right hand since he had never regained feeling in his left. He presented me a small black case with a photo of Oscar and Shakespeare that he'd attached to the cover. Inside was a collection of twelve CD's that he'd burnt, all filled with his favorite songs.

We thanked Kurt for the present and retreated to the kitchen behind the altar once more. The guests had begun to trickle in, and I really didn't want to mingle this close to the start of the wedding ceremony. Bruce and I made the last-minute decision as to who would enter on which side of the altar: we'd already nixed the idea of walking down the aisle early in our planning. In one commitment ceremony we had attended, the grooms walked together down the aisle of Arlington Street Church. That affair boasted a guest list four times the size of ours and was complete with evergreen garlands draped along the pews and sprays of candles throughout the church. Ours hardly warranted the formality of a wedding march. Besides, the last thing I wanted that day was to be stared at for what I'm sure would seem like hours on end.

I left Bruce alone in a room off the kitchen that led to the right front of the church. I stayed in the minister's study which led to the left. Our cue for entering was the opening words to the first hymn, "Make Channels for the Streams of Love," which the music director of the church was to play on the organ. I'd originally thought the piano to be a better accompaniment for our service, but Bruce had always loved the majestic sound of the organ. As I listened to Rose play the introduction, I decided Bruce was right: the organ did add a stately tone to the service. I had spent so much time downplaying the ceremonial aspect of the wedding that I was glad Bruce had insisted on some degree of grandeur.

I loved that we had decided to have the guests sing rather than hire someone to sing for us, but I was petrified I'd do something wrong. Maybe I'd misunderstood and we were supposed to enter on the *last* words of the hymn. What if I walked into the sanctuary, only to stand by myself at the altar for three full verses?

I willed myself to open the door, turned immediately to my right, and was relieved to see that Bruce was not only facing me, but that we'd timed our entrances perfectly. We met each other front and center of the altar, climbed three stairs, and smiled at Jane, who was waiting for us. When the hymn ended, she said the first words of the service:

> We are here to abet creation and
> To witness to it,
> To notice each other's beautiful
> Face and complex nature
> So that creation need not play to
> An empty house.

She proceeded to light a candle with the words: "On this day, the birthday of the Rev. Dr. Martin Luther King, Jr., we light a candle in gratitude for all those with us and before us who have given of themselves so that we might all live in a more equitable world."

Jane then talked about marriage to the two of us. One of the thoughts that has stayed with me was her view that "marriage symbolizes the sharing of two lives." I'd never really considered marriage as a symbol before; I thought I was protesting for a *right* not a *symbol*. But Jane's words made sense: symbols of our society are some of the most powerful ways we have to communicate. We do, indeed, fight for symbols. Every once in a while, an amendment to outlaw flag-burning surfaced because this symbol was so meaningful in our culture. I was ready to think about marriage as a symbol now, too. It wasn't just the *ring* that was a symbol, marriage itself was. It symbolized love, commitment, and the creation of a new entity: we.

I also liked that Jane spoke of marriage in realistic, rather than romantic, terms. She said, "We must give ourselves in love, but we must not give ourselves away." I thought that Bruce and I did quite well in this area. I don't think either one of us considered marriage as giving ourselves away. We had been able to achieve a relationship that allowed each of us to grow.

Our friend Francie, whose wedding we had attended the previous summer, read Mary Oliver's "Wild Geese." We sang another hymn, and our friend Jen delivered the reading by Carter Heyward. I tried to remember the advice Bruce had given me to always look at him or the person who was speaking, but I had a difficult time keeping my focus. I looked out over the audience, picking out the faces of people I hadn't seen for years as well as the ones I'd just seen yesterday. Finally we came to the exchange of the vows and rings. I wasn't used to expressing emotion in front of people, and had been worried that the intensity of feeling might overwhelm me, so I spoke softly at first, growing in volume as I became more certain of myself:

> In reaffirming the relationship we have been building,
> I, Ken, take you, Bruce, to be my spouse,
> Together to love, to work, and to share,
> To grow and to understand,
> To discover a deeper, fuller life.

Bruce repeated the vow, his eyes fixed on mine. He's better at this, I thought; he's always been the less inhibited of the two of us. I tried not to feel self-conscious, and for the most part I succeeded, but throughout the ceremony I was intermittently aware of standing in front of a church full of people.

It was time to exchange the rings we had privately exchanged five years earlier. We had decided to wear our rings on the traditional third finger, left hand, after having worn them on our third finger, right. We wanted to acknowledge that our relationship had changed – at least in name – with our marriage, and this seemed like a subtle way to do it. The words we spoke were simple yet summed up precisely what the rings mean to us:

> I give you this ring
> To wear upon your hand
> As a symbol of our love.

When Bruce went to place the ring on my finger it got stuck, and I spent the next few minutes trying to twist the band over my knuckle. It was the sort of mishap the Jerry Falwells of the world would have pointed to as a sign of God's wrath at our marriage.

Bruce and I had discussed at length how Jane would pronounce us married. We didn't want to be husband and husband, but we did want the legality of our marriage to be clear. Our solution wasn't terribly imaginative, but managed to reflect both our commitment to each other and the legal status of us as a couple. Jane's voice trembled as she began: "By the power vested in me by the state of Massachusetts, I now pronounce you spouses for life." She had to pause briefly mid sentence to gain her composure. I, too, could feel the tears well up and was glad I didn't have to speak again. When I looked at Bruce, his eyes were moist.

I had been especially nervous about the kiss that followed the vows. I realized that many of the straight people in the church would not have seen two men kiss – or at least not very often – and I was angry at myself for thinking about how comfortable people would be. It wasn't until later that I understood that I was doing these friends of ours a grave injustice: Seeing the two of us kiss would *not* have made them uncomfortable. They were on our side. But years of defensiveness ran deep. I'd been let down by people I'd trusted to be open-minded about who I was, and I found it hard to accept that the people who sat in the church deserved trust.

Our kiss was quick, a congenial peck on the lips followed by an embrace. This felt right to me even if I hadn't had difficulties trusting my friends. I'd never felt comfortable touching or kissing in public; I even had a hard time of it in the Castro District in San Francisco where just about everyone was gay. Bruce and I clung to each other longer than I'd expected. When we let go, I was startled by the burst of applause from the sanctuary. Bruce and I turned to the guests and smiled; they continued clapping. Some were crying.

"We'll Build a Land," our exit hymn, was the most overtly political piece of the ceremony. It resonated with the idealism of the sixties, calling for building a land of peace where the broken are bound up and captives were freed and where justice would "roll down like waters." It seemed a fitting end to the service, and it was one of my favorite hymns. I was used to singing it in the pews with the congregation but now, on the altar, the sound was rich and full. I stood for a moment, holding hands with Bruce, and basked in the music.

After the first verse we walked down the aisle, smiling to the guests as we passed them. We stood at the door of the church to receive people. Ed was one of the first to greet us; he'd begun to walk toward the back of the church during the last stanza of the hymn. Bruce and I hugged him tightly; he was the closest thing to family we had in the audience.

The guests streamed out, each hugging us, kissing us, and holding our hands. Some of our friends were still crying openly. The mother of one of my students the previous year tried to speak but burst into tears. "I'm so sorry," she said. "I never cry at weddings. Never. But this was just overwhelming."

I believe that much of the beauty of the service was, of course, in seeing two people who were dear to her wed. But there was also an underlying sadness to much of the reaction I felt as people exited. The sense that we have so far to go before we are a truly equitable society seemed to permeate the church. None of the guests knew if this marriage they had just witnessed would be allowed to stay intact.

It took us almost an hour to greet everyone in the church. It wasn't the numbers that made the greeting long – we could have perfunctorily greeted everyone in ten minutes or so – it was how everyone wanted to talk with us, simply *be* with us. We were a reception line of two and, unlike longer lines in larger, more traditional weddings, all the guests knew who they were greeting. No Aunt Sadies or Uncle Rays whom no one had seen in decades. It was just the two of us, and people wanted to stay for a moment, congratulate us on our marriage. Very few in the church had ever attended a same-sex wedding, and although I know that people were deeply moved by Bruce and me, they were also experiencing an emotional first.

I was glad people took their time with us. I needed our friends to show their support and love. It was at this point in the wedding when, happy as I was to finally be married, I felt the absence of family: my sister and mother, aunts and uncles, Bruce's father, and, most keenly, Bruce's daughters. Of course it wasn't *my* mother I was missing, but rather the mother I wished I'd had, the mother who'd accepted who I was and could be happy for me.

When we finished our greetings, Bruce and I drove the few blocks back to our house, where the street was lined with cars. We parked on a side street and for a moment, as we walked toward the porch, I felt a bit like a guest myself, eager to see the married couple. This feeling was reinforced when a woman from the catering staff took our coats at the door and put them on the bed upstairs. I was relieved to see that there was indeed plenty of room for all our guests. I had been worried that everyone would be squeezed elbow to elbow, barely able to lift their drinks.

I don't remember much about the reception except that it was easier than I'd thought. It was *fun*, something I never would have believed possible with our obligations to talk to every guest for at least a minute or two. People laughed, hugged us, talked to each other, drank, sampled food, and admired the house and the flower blanket across the fireplace mantel. A few friends had bought disposable cameras, and were busy taking pictures of the party.

I reacquainted with old college friends, former teaching colleagues, and people I'd not been in touch with for quite some time, while Bruce made the rounds with his colleagues from work and members of our congregation at First Parish. I was touched by the good wishes, most of which weren't any different from what you'd hear at any wedding. But there was one that recognized the unique nature of the service has stayed with me.

Martin is the husband of a friend of mine at school. He's a faithful Catholic, but a progressive one, liberal on social issues. I approached him and Abby to thank them for coming and for their blessings, but Martin's comment took me aback.

"You know how some people oppose gay marriage to 'protect the sanctity of marriage'?" he asked. "Well, after that ceremony I feel like the sanctity of my marriage has deepened."

I'd never thought about our marrying in quite those terms. I was used to rebutting – even in my imagination while listening to the talking heads on TV – that my marriage couldn't possibly weaken someone else's. But I'd never considered that my marriage to Bruce would actually strengthen the institution of marriage. Martin was right. When people try to overcome obstacle after obstacle to *be* married, the institution itself is more deeply appreciated.

Toward the end of the reception, the caterers called everyone into the dining room for the cutting of the cake. We'd opted out of the groom and groom statuettes in favor of real flowers to decorate the single tier with white frosting. Once everyone had gathered, Bruce began to speak. I thought it would be a quick toast and thank you, but instead he talked about his own foibles and my supposed patience with him in the wittiest of terms. He ended by saying that he was so glad to be spending his life with me and told me that he loved me. I hadn't thought at all about what to say and couldn't come close to matching him, so I just expressed my love and happiness to be spending my life with him, too. Everyone clinked champagne glasses and the afternoon began to wind to a close.

Before everyone left, though, Oscar and Shakespeare snuck out of the guest room and bounced down the stairs to the first floor. The sedatives had begun to wear off, and they darted about legs, just out of my reach. I was worried they'd sneak out of the house as people were leaving, so I enlisted some friends to help me grab the dogs by the collars and drag them back upstairs. When the minor chaos had abated, one friend of mine said, "Okay. Forget the ceremony. Forget the toasts. *That* was marriage. You spend months planning the perfect wedding and the image I'll always remember of this day is you chasing a couple of basset hounds around the house in your snazzy new suit."

"Hey, didn't we forget something?" Jane said from the couch. "I still need to sign the marriage certificate." She removed the document and a pen from her bag while I grabbed a camera from a friend. She signed it with great flare and an even greater smile. It was a formality, of course, one that I knew wouldn't erase the image of me chasing the dogs, but I wanted a picture nonetheless. It was official. We were man and man, husband and husband, spouses for life.

We were married in the state of Massachusetts.

By the end of the day we were tired: I from three straight hours social obligation and Bruce from his usual need for more sleep than he'd had the night before. We coaxed the dogs to their couch in the kitchen, where they fell immediately to sleep. Bruce and I retreated to our bedroom for a nap.

I wrapped my arms around Bruce who was on his side with his back to me. It was our usual sleeping position, one that he loved. I always had a difficult time being the held one: some primal fear in me arose each time he tried to hold me from behind. He whispered his usual "This feels nice," before he drifted off. I stayed awake and held him, falling into rhythm with his breath.

We're not leaving. Any fear that Bruce and I might leave each other was not rational. There had been no fights of the kind when one of us stormed out of the house in a huff. We'd easily followed the old advice about never going to bed mad. But lying there next to him, officially married, I found myself drifting into a deeper feeling of security, and then into sleep.

I woke up before Bruce, an hour or so later, and rolled on my side. I pulled his arms around me so that he rolled over, too.

He held me. I closed my eyes.

"It's time to leave for our honeymoon," Bruce whispered.

To say that we could have walked to our honeymoon destination is not at all an exaggeration. We *would* have walked to the restaurant, but it was bitter cold that night. We decided to drive around the corner instead. We'd never been to Il Capriccio but had heard about it many times. It was hard to find even though it was on Main Street since its sign was barely visible and it unobtrusively abutted a liquor store. It was known as one of the best restaurants in the Boston area, however, and was always packed. Entering the restaurant was how I imagined it might have been entering a speak-easy. The absence of windows and the dim lighting created a clandestine feel to the place. Inside it was pulsating with life. Laughter erupted from the bar where customers waited for their tables; waiters carried trays of Northern Italian food high above their heads.

We'd reserved a table in the quieter section of the restaurant but hadn't explained that this was our wedding night meal. I suppose it would have been natural for a newlywed couple to have offered this information, but I wanted to avoid even the possibility of public attention. I also didn't want a reason to be annoyed that evening, and this meant not giving anyone the opportunity to question who we were. This was our evening and ours alone. We didn't need to educate.

The menu was immense: three-, four-, five-course meals of every Italian dish imaginable. We ordered extravagantly and ate rather sparingly; this evening was not about the food. We toasted ourselves and our lives together, expressed our love for each other, our happiness at being married. We told each other how lucky we were to have met each other. It was a quiet meal but the silences weren't awkward. We were completely at ease. It was just another meal together and yet it was the most important meal of our lives: the first as a married couple. When we requested a container to take the leftovers back to Oscar and Shakespeare, I wondered aloud how many honeymoons ended with a doggie bag.

We left the restaurant happy and tired, then drove around the block to spend our wedding night in the same bed we had shared for many years.

CHAPTER SEVENTEEN

ALL OVER THE MAP

Shortly after the wedding, Bruce sunk into a depression. I'd heard of post-partum depressions but never of post-*nuptial* depressions. I'd seen Bruce in a depression — just as he'd seen me — but this was one of the worst. When I came home from school today to find him still in bed at 4:30 p.m., I pushed the issue.

"What's going on?" I asked.

"I just decided to work from home," Bruce said, ignoring the contradiction between his use of the word "work" and being in bed.

"How are you? Tell me."

"Okay."

We both were used to playing the "okay" game. You pronounced the two syllables with the tonal nuance of native Chinese speakers to convey a range of meanings from "Okay, but there's no way you should believe me," to "Okay. Fine. What about you?"

Bruce's "okay" was clearly not your ordinary "I'm doing just fine."

"I don't believe you," I said.

"I'm sort of down," he finally said.

My response to his feeling low was almost always to review my actions of the last few weeks to uncover something I'd said or done wrong.

It dawned on me that I'd recently *married* him; I was hoping my misstep was more along the lines of a thoughtless comment about the Tamale Pie he'd made for dinner the other night.

"Is it me?" I asked. "Something I said? Something I did?"

"No, Honey," Bruce said. "It's not you."

I was absolutely horrible when it came to not knowing the truth about something that affected me. I should have given Bruce space, believed him when he told me I hadn't caused him any pain.

I should have remembered that his daughter had been hospitalized a little over a month ago.

"I think this Kate situation has finally caught up with me," Bruce said. His voice began to quaver; his eyes became watery.

"I'm sorry," I said. "I'm really sorry. And I'm sorry I took the whole thing to myself. I should have known that sooner or later you'd crash about Kate."

Bruce looked at me. "To be honest," he said, "I'm not sure how I would have made it *without* the wedding. I think that's what kept me going. I know you sometimes thought I wasn't as invested as I should be. But it really saved me, Ken. It's what got me through these weeks."

I hugged him. I didn't say anything. I just held him, let him know I was there for him.

Bruce turned 48 about a month after that conversation. He was doing better with the help of a therapist I'd suggested. A change of medications, a little less travel, and Kate's improved health also helped.

We celebrated his birthday with a quiet dinner out. Neither of us liked big parties in our honor – and I didn't really like it party for that matter – and this was a perfect way to mark the occasion. We went to a small Thai restaurant a few blocks from our house called the Tree Top. It was a family-run business. That night one of the children was coloring on a table in the corner while an older one was doing homework. But it was also a romantic place – lights dim, candles, good wine, a table away from anyone's earshot. What a feat to be both a family business *and* romantic at the same time. I was looking forward to Kate's moving in with us, but I also hoped that we could strike that same balance of family and romance.

Politically, we were still in marital limbo in Massachusetts. The backstage political drama was beginning anew, with many gay marriage opponents withdrawing support from any constitutional amendment that included provisions for ensuring any rights for same-sex couples. Another amendment was starting to take shape that would ban same-sex marriage, period. No guaranteed civil unions. No guaranteed hospital visitation rights. Some legal scholars believed that this new amendment might even make any sort of gay union unconstitutional. No one seemed to be able to get an accurate head count of legislators if the amendment were to come to a vote, so the constitutional convention was put off for a while.

Future presidential candidate Mitt Romney – a man who could raise my blood pressure faster than a space shuttle at liftoff – used his opposition to marriage equality to rally the conservative base of the national Republican Party. In a speech in South Carolina, he boasted that he not only was fighting gay marriage in Massachusetts, but that he also opposed changing birth certificates to read "parent/parent" rather than "mother/father," a policy under consideration to accommodate the new inclusive reality in the state. "It's not right on paper: it's not right in fact," he told the crowd and C-Span viewers. He also feigned shock when he said that gay couples "are actually having children born to them." In Utah he told an audience that the very fact that Massachusetts allowed gay couples to marry was weakening the reputation of the United States as a world leader. It was clear that opposing gay marriage was going to be a cornerstone of his presidential campaign.

By the spring of 2005, the legality of same-sex marriage had by now begun to reach the courts and legislatures in other states. Some were discovering that the sweeping bans on gay marriage in the November elections were harming more than gay people. Utah legislators revisited their ban when they realized the measure could deny hospital visitation rights to grandparents or siblings. Still, lawmakers feared that any easing of restrictions would be the first step to gay marriage, and the rigid amendment remained intact. And in Florida, the first attempt to require recognition of a same-sex marriage outside Massachusetts failed when a judge ruled that refusing to honor the out-of-state marriage was not discriminatory.

I searched through dictionaries trying to find one definition of *discrimination* that would help me make sense of this ruling. I couldn't even find one. Instead, all the entries supported the notion that bias – not fairness – was at the heart of the judge's thinking.

While the news from states like Florida was deeply dishearten-ing, at least Connecticut provided us with a little hope when Governor Jodi Rell, a Republican, signed into the law the first civil unions bill to be enacted without prompting from the courts. Recognition of same-sex couples in Vermont and Massachusetts was a result of court action. This time, the legislature was ahead of the game: by an impressive majority, both the Connecticut senate and house quietly approved what had been so controversial only five years ago.

I suppose I should have been more grateful for this turn of events, but a last-minute amendment to the bill left me with a bitter aftertaste. The law specifically stated that marriage – *the real deal* – was an institution exclusively for heterosexual couples. It didn't matter that this was already Connecticut law. Did the legislature think we needed reminding? That we would forget that this was the case in every other state except Massachu-setts?

Although she was clearly disappointed that Connecticut went the "separate but equal" route to recognition rather than granting full mar-riage rights in substance and in name, Mary Bonauto reminded us how different the landscape was now as opposed to only a year ago. I tried to listen to her voice more, to consider the bigger picture. After all, if anyone had the right to speak with moral authority on the issue was the attorney who argued the marriage cases in both Vermont and Massachusetts. And it was always possible that this legislation would be a stepping stone to full marriage rights, which would make the pill much easier to swallow.

That spring Kansas became the eighteenth state to incorporate the exclusion of gay couples from marriage in its constitution. Sixteen other states were seriously considering similar action. Perhaps the only positive side of this wave of anti-gay sentiment was that there would now be official documents that some day would tell the true history of what was happening in the country right at the time. I was a teacher who used original texts all the time. To teach about anti-Chinese sentiment in the late 1800's, all I had to do is show political cartoons of the period along with some legal documents. I found myself imagining life some years from now. I imagined a young teacher showing these marriage amendments along with the writing of their supporters as evidence that we'd yet to learn all the lessons we were supposed to from history. In my more optimistic moments, I pictured myself teaching with these texts.

Maryland passed a more limited bill than Connecticut's that would allow couples who register to make medical decisions for each other. And New Jersey was considering a bill that, like Maryland's law, would be limited in scope, while the issue of granting marriage licenses to gay couples was making its way through the state's court system. Oregon, too, was considering a bill that would grant rights to gay couples.

Sometimes I felt like I needed a scorecard or a map of the United States, like the ones used to record electoral votes in a presidential election, just to keep track of where Bruce and I were a couple, where we might be a couple, or where we had no rights as a couple whatsoever. It felt like having multiple identities.

CHAPTER EIGHTEEN

HONEYMOON

Shortly after our wedding I received word that the short-story collection published in 2000 would be translated into Italian. The offer came out of the blue; I had no idea any negotiations were even taking place. The Italian publisher asked if Bruce and I could fly to Italy for a small publicity tour: Rome, Padua, Bologna, and Ferrera. We decided to extend the trip and call it a honeymoon, since we didn't have the chance to get away after we were married last January.

We stopped in London on the way to Rome, where we saw theater, went to bookstores and museums. I dragged Bruce to 84 Charing Cross Road, the site of the bookstore of Helene Hanff's memoir in letters named after the address. For years she had written to the proprietor of the second-hand bookstore there, and published her charming correspondence. I had heard that the bookstore had closed, but what I didn't expect was what had been put in its place: a pizza joint. I guess I really am a romantic at heart; I felt as if I were returning to a childhood home that had been demolished to build more profitable town houses. And this over a place I had only visited in letters. No one can tell me a piece of paper doesn't matter.

We spent a good deal of time with the publisher and the translator, but we also had romantic dinners on the sidewalks of Rome. The final night, the publisher staged an event in a popular bookstore, where an Italian actor read one of my stories and an Italian writer who translates Michael Cunningham's work gave a short talk on my writing. Of course I couldn't understand most of what he said, so the translator summed up for me at the end of his lecture. The height of the evening came after the presentations, when the publisher brought out bottles of champagne to toast our marriage. The audience cheered.

On the plane home from Italy, we were given two separate customs cards to fill out. We had no box to identify our relationship: we weren't married in the US government's eyes, so we were reduced to roommates living in the same house.

"I hate this," I said to Bruce. "One minute we're married and the next minute we're not."

"We'll be in Massachusetts soon," Bruce said. "Then we'll be legal again."

"Until we go to New Hampshire," I said. "Or Canada. Or New York City. Or –

"I know," Bruce said. "I get it. I really do."

The second leg of our honeymoon was Canada. Although our marriage was not legal there – the Canadian government will only acknowledge agreements recognized by the *federal* government of the United States – Canadian officials *usually* treated it as such. They allow us to fill out one form, check off the word "married," and pass through customs together. We were treated respectfully.

Not so this time.

"What do you mean you are *married*?" said the customs officer, a woman in her sixties. She shook her head. "That is *impossible*."

"Well, we are," I said.

"Two men can not get married in the United States," she said. The disgust in her voice was startling.

"We were married in January, 2005," Bruce said.

"Where?" she demanded. "What state are you from?"

"Massachusetts," I said. "Two men *can* get married there."

"Well, you're not married here," she said. She stamped our papers and, still shaking her head, pointed toward the exit to the baggage terminal.

We were relieved to arrive in Stratford, a small town with a significant gay population and many gay-friendly businesses. After we unpacked, Bruce took a nap and I went out to the wraparound porch of the bed and breakfast. I had been reading in the rocker for about hour or so, interrupted only when I looked up to watch a bicyclist coast by.

The screen door opened, and Bruce appeared bearing a bottle of white wine and two glasses. A book was wedged under his arm.

"Mind if I join you?"

"Of course you can," I said, patting the seat of the rocker next too me.

He sat and poured us wine. He raised his glass to clink against mine.

"You're very sweet," I said.

"To being here," he said, and held up his glass in a toast.

He opened his book. We flipped our feet up on the railing and began to read. It felt like the height of decadence: a late-afternoon glass of wine and leisurely reading on a weekday.

"That customs official was something, wasn't she?" I said.

"Maybe we should go to City Hall today. That way they'd never question us again." He swirled the last of his wine and drank it. "It's four 'o clock. I think they're open until five o'clock."

We walked to City Hall, a massive red-brick Victorian building in the center of Stratford. A receptionist informed us that marriage licenses were issued on the bottom floor.

The room was empty. We explained to the woman behind the counter that we would like to marry. She gave us no double-take, no expression of either pleasure or displeasure. I liked this neutrality and remembered the Norman Rockwell painting called "The Marriage License" that hung over the desk at the Waltham licensing office: two young white blonds, man and woman of course, filling out their forms while an elderly clerk looks on. There were no paintings in Stratford; it was all business here.

The woman handed us some forms. "When do you plan to marry?"

"Maybe in October," Bruce says. "Columbus Day weekend. We're from the United States."

"That shouldn't be a problem," she said. "Neither of you has been married before, right?"

"I am divorced," Bruce said.

"Well, that's going to complicate matters," the woman said matter-of-factly. "You're going to have to hire a Canadian lawyer who will verify your divorce. You'll need to present your divorce papers. Then your lawyer will write an official letter."

We had almost missed our flight to Toronto because Bruce couldn't find his passport. We had turned the house upside down, had gone to his office, to our safe deposit box at the bank, then back home for one more look. He finally found his birth certificate, which would suffice.

He'll never find the divorce papers, I thought.

"Don't worry," the woman said. "It'll take awhile, but you can get it done. Perhaps even by October."

We left the office and descended the wide front steps that fanned onto the sidewalk. Bruce sat with me on a step.

"Will this ever get any easier?" I asked him. "It's just one obstacle after another."

Bruce rubbed my back. "We'll get married in Canada," he said, ever the optimist. "Don't worry. It'll happen."

It occurred to me we'd always be working to make sure we could stay married and that our status didn't change because we were flying over a state that didn't consider our relationship valid.

Bruce stood. "Come on," he said. "Let's take a walk along the Avon River. Then we can have dinner."

He reached down and I grabbed his hand, then he slowly pulled me up.

CHAPTER NINETEEN

IN SICKNESS AND IN HEALTH

With the second Massachusetts Constitutional Convention on hold, I had to put my political energies elsewhere. Shortly after we returned from our honeymoon in the summer of 2005, I read about a candidate for Governor of Massachusetts, an African American man who was Assistant Attorney General in the Clinton administration. Deval Patrick was hardly a household name, but everything he said rang true to me. He was completely in favor of marriage equality. He spoke about building community, about working for the common good. I signed on immediately.

A few months later, Bruce and I hosted a community meeting to help organize the campaign. Patrick was still the longest of long shots, but the enthusiasm in our house that evening was inspiring. I decided to run for a delegate seat at the State Democratic Convention in the caucuses that winter. In my speech at the caucus, I hardly played my cards close to my chest. While the other candidates were temperate in their remarks – either claiming neutrality for candidates or, in the case of one, suggesting that he "finds himself agreeing with much of what Deval Patrick says" – I stood up and said, "I'm here only because of Deval Patrick and especially his support of gay marriage." I guess that every worthwhile cause has to have its supporters with tunnel-vision, the ones who keep their eyes on the prize, who keep pointing ahead when people are looking the other way. I felt a little silly about my speech; I knew that there were other issues and, contrary to what Bruce teasingly said to me, I would not vote for Newt Gingrich if he suddenly supported gay marriage yet kept all his other positions.

That spring, I found myself at the convention in Worcester. We handily nominated Deval Patrick our candidate for governor. I had never been to a political convention before, let alone gone as a delegate. Just about every candidate at the convention mentioned same-sex-marriage rights in their speeches, although some more enthusiastically than others. But whatever the tone, the words were greeted with a roaring ovation. It was no longer political suicide to support gay marriage, at least not among Democrats. Four years ago only one candidate for governor, Robert Reich, took this position, which was at the time seen as an extreme political risk. By spring of 2005 it looked like it would be political suicide to oppose it.

Once nominations were decided and acceptance speeches were made, the convention recessed until Sunday. I went with another delegate from my district to a party hosted by MassEquality, the group that was working for same-sex marriage in the state. It was comforting to be in a roomful of mostly gay people. I even recognized some of them from the hours we spent in front of the State House during the constitutional conventions. But after a while, I grew tired. I missed Bruce, and looked forward to our late-night chat. It was a strange role rehearsal: He was usually the one away from home.

I was surprised that he didn't answer when I phoned and hoped I wasn't waking him up with my midnight call. Then the answering machine kicked in with a new message, "I tried to call you on your cell but couldn't get you. I'm fine. Just call this number."

I had no idea where I was calling, but Bruce picked up.

"I didn't want to worry you. I'm fine. I had some chest pains and went to the emergency ward. They wanted to keep me under observation until the morning. I'll be home before noon."

Of course I didn't believe that he was fine, and insisted on coming home at once, but he talked sense into me. He was going to sleep and I was only an hour away. Everything was fine, but even if it wasn't, I could get to the hospital quickly.

"This always happens, you know," I said.

"What happens?"

"One of us gets sick when the other is away." I cited a list of examples as proof positive that there was something mysterious about the way we either were hurt or fell ill when apart: heart palpitations, stitches, a broken hand, a broken collarbone, trouble breathing.

"I guess we just shouldn't be apart," Bruce said.

"Sounds good to me."

I relaxed when I hung up. When either of us got sick, we worried about what role we'd be allowed to play in decision-making or whether we'd be able to visit. Now that we were married in Massachusetts that wasn't a problem, but who knew what would happen if we were in other places we'd visited together: Dallas, New Orleans, St. Louis?

I let my thoughts drift away from Bruce – he was going to be fine – and focused on how much I needed this weekend at the Convention. The US Senate was soon to vote on a constitutional amendment to ban gay marriage. The vote would fall far short of the 2/3 needed to pass – a majority of senators didn't even support it – but that there was even a vote was frightening nonetheless. Only three other countries had written such language into their constitutions and one of them – Uganda – was known to have executed people for having gay sex. Senate Majority Leader Bill Frist called the vote even though he knew he was well short of the necessary support. It was all a rather cynical, exploitative ploy to get senators on record as opposing the amendment so gay marriage could be used once again as a divisive issue in this fall's campaigns. Even given the disappointments of the past few years, I still found it staggering how easily and callously politicians would play with people's very lives in an effort to gain power.

But for now I reminded myself to be happy that the Democratic State Convention had gone well. More importantly, Bruce was going to be fine. It was a false alarm. Not long after his trip to the emergency ward came mine. This time the alarm was the real thing.

I had promised Charlotte that I would take her to see the musical *Avenue Q* when it came to Boston. It was an unabashed bribe to get her to finish an English paper. I remember giving her a lineup of bribes, one for each page. A trip to a bookstore, a movie, the play. I might have even offered her money. Anyway, it worked. She finished the paper before dinner.

Bruce and I decided to make it a threesome: Charlotte and "the daddies," as she called us. We bought matinee tickets for a Saturday. We'd go to the show, then go out to dinner in Boston, anyplace that had great hamburgers, the staple of Charlotte's diet. As usual Willa, the basset puppy we bought after Oscar went to his reward, woke us up early–about six – and we had our breakfast and read the paper. I was reminded of a wonderful quote by Anne Morrow Lindbergh: "A simple enough pleasure, surely, to have breakfast alone with one's husband, but how seldom married people in the midst of life achieve it." Well, on that morning, at least, we had achieved it.

I was the first to shower, since I had volunteered to pick Charlotte up at her mother's house. I will never forget the moment when my hand went numb. I was washing my hair, and my initial reaction was that I had mistakenly massaged some of Kate's shampoo into my scalp, some sort of menthol product that had left my hand tingling. When I removed my hand from my head and the tingling had turned to numbness, I knew something was very wrong. I tried to pick up a towel, but couldn't feel it and it dropped to the floor. I dressed quickly, unable to zip up the fly of my jeans – a two-handed endeavor.

I ran downstairs. Bruce was cleaning up the kitchen.

"Something is really wrong," I said, then went on to describe my symptoms. We decided right then to go to the emergency ward.

In the car, some feeling came back for a few moments, but then my hand became numb again. I spent much of the ten-minute ride trying to convince myself aloud that the numbness could be carpel-tunnel syndrome, a pinched nerve, or some minor ailment I'd never heard of. Bruce tried to calm me by agreeing that my initial diagnosis of this being a serious matter might have been premature.

The first thing the receptionist asked me was if I'd ever had a stroke. I told him that I hadn't, but this didn't seem to make him any less concerned. He whisked Bruce and me into the triage station ahead of everyone else. A nurse took my blood pressure, temperature, and oxygen level while she talked. I'm sure her bright tone was meant to calm me, but it had the opposite effect: I couldn't help but think she had decided I needed to get my mind off something horrible.

She then sat at her computer and asked enough questions to pull up my file from previous trips to the hospital ward on her screen. She double-checked a few facts about my insurance and religious affiliation before she came to the question about next of kin.

I couldn't remember a time when the word I was about to say was so important to me. Even using it at our wedding didn't measure up to this moment. If it is ever possible to actually *feel* a word, I did.

"Bruce is my husband," I said.

The nurse didn't miss a beat when she asked for Bruce's full name. No second look, no story about her gay cousin, no request to repeat my answer. It was refreshing for this to be so normal: *husband* communicated to her layers of cultural and emotional meaning. From this one word she was able to understand how much we meant to each other, that Bruce was to be in on all the decisions, that he would be at my bedside as long as he needed to be, that he was, well, my *husband.*

It was the first of many times I would say the word that day. We'd been legally married for quite some time, but it was as if the word had just been given to me. I said it with the frequency that couples say *I love you* those first days after one of them takes the plunge and first announces his feelings. But the effect was immediate: those around me began to use the words as well.

"I need to talk to you and your husband," my doctor said in the emergency ward after a CT scan and an MRI. Bruce came in from where he was standing, just outside the room.

"What's wrong?" I asked.

"You've had a stroke. Three of them, in fact. Small ones, all probably the result of the same clot. You're going to have to stay here for a few days of tests and observation. We'll talk about any rehabilitation later."

I looked at my husband. We were both stunned. I was only fifty years old, had perfect blood pressure, was in reasonably good shape, and had a cholesterol level many people envy. What was going on here?

"It could be lots of things," the doctor said, "but at your age it's probably a condition a lot of people have where there's a small hole in one of the heart valves. We'll need to do an ultrasound to see if that's what's wrong. We can fix it pretty easily."

"That doesn't *sound* very easy to fix," I said.

"It's the same thing that happened to Teddy Bruschi."

I'd never heard of Teddy Bruschi, which my face must clearly have communicated.

"You know, Teddy Bruschi," the doctor explained. "The football player who had the stroke a few years back."

"Of course," I said, pretending to know who he was talking about. I was momentarily proud of the macho male bonding I'd faked my way through until I realized again what was happening. A stroke.

They gave me some medication and moved me into a semi-private room with an elderly man who had also suffered a stroke, far worse than mine. Once I settled in, Bruce left to bring me some essentials from home: books, my laptop, pajama bottoms so I wouldn't have to stay in the paper-thin smock they had given me. I began to regain some feeling in my arm and didn't feel sick in the least. When the doctors asked me to demonstrate strength in my right arm by pushing hard against their splayed hands, they were pleased.

I turned on the TV to watch the political news on CNN, but couldn't focus. Easter was the next day, and when I realized I wouldn't be home, I saddened. Christmas wasn't the only holiday Bruce and I had redefined since we'd met. Easter, too, was a big day, and tomorrow Beth, her boyfriend, her cousin, Charlotte, Kate, and a friend were supposed to join Bruce and me for a mid-afternoon lunch.

Since I couldn't come to Easter, Easter came to me. The entourage arrived after everyone had finished their meal. Charlotte gave me a chocolate bunny and some Peeps. Beth brought some magazines. Beth's cousin – a real Patriots fan – entered holding up her Teddy Bruschi sweatshirt that she offered as a get-well gift. Mary Louise is as down-to-earth as you can get. She moonlights tending bar, a job that seems perfect for her extroverted nature. I imagine her booming laugh can be heard even above the din of night-club chatter and music. I took the opportunity to ask her more about Bruschi; she was surprisingly well informed about his health.

The doctors performed more tests the next day – an echo-cardiagram and something called a trans-esophogeal echo-cardiagram – that failed to reveal that Mr. Bruschi and I shared anything more than the state of Massachusetts. Bruce picked me up later that day. I left with instructions to take 325 mg of aspirin every morning and to make follow-up appointments with my primary care doctor and the neurologist who treated me in the hospital.

I left the hospital with my husband, his arm tightly linked to mine. We walked slowly to the car. I couldn't wait to get home.

I recovered from the stroke completely, although only a few weeks later I encountered another medical issue: a detached retina that required five surgeries. For months after the surgeries I had no sight in my right eye. It then started to slowly return. The doctor told me that it could come back more in time – perhaps months or years,

As was true when I had the stroke, Bruce's role as my husband allowed him to be at my side through all the surgeries and endless medical appointments. The opthamologists treated the two of us with nothing but respect. The surgeons gave Bruce information reserved for family members. Being married made a difference.

I also found myself more willing to ask for help from my friends. Joan Wickersham was a godsend, filling in when Bruce was away, driving me to appointments and surgeries, visiting with lunch, and watching *Sex and the City* reruns with me. She offered help and I asked for it. What struck me was how easily I was able to ask for help; I rarely ask people to do anything for me. Part of my comfort level, of course, was who Joan is, but there was another piece. Now, married, when I asked for help, I felt like I was asking people to step in temporarily. I felt less needy as a married person, and this truth allowed me to reach out to friends knowing that there was no suggestion of a lengthy commitment. Not that any of them would have shied away from helping me even if it did mean protracted caretaking. The point is I was more comfortable asking for help knowing I had a husband who had vowed to care for me as I would for him.

The effects of marriage continue to surprise me.

CHAPTER TWENTY

ONWARD

The debate over marriage equality is slowly shifting our way, despite some setbacks. Six states have or will soon have same-sex marriage: Maine, Vermont, Connecticut, New Hampshire, Iowa and, of course, Massachusetts. Perhaps even more indicative of our success is that in three of these states, marriage was granted not by the courts but by the legislature. Two governors signed the bills. Vermont Governor Jim Douglas vetoed the legislation, but his veto was overridden. It is no longer political suicide to support gay marriage. In some places, it's political suicide not to.

I was at the mall not too long ago and walked past a long table with petitions and pens strewn across it. A sign was draped that read "Let the People Vote." It was an anti-gay-marriage petition drive. It seemed out of place; Massachusetts resolved the issue a long time ago.

The two volunteers at the table in the mall wouldn't agree, of course. They stood by their table, smiling to passers-by, selecting their prospective signers carefully. I know. I watched them. Why was I so obsessed? I took the escalator to the second level of the mall and looked over the railing to see how many people they could get to sign. They approached older people, couples that were clearly heterosexual as they held hands or pushed their strollers. I felt as if I were doing something illegal, as if someone might be watching me as I made a mental tally of how many takers the petitioners could boast in ten minutes.

One.

Most people showed some initial interest. Why not let the people vote? That's what democracy is all about, isn't it? But it was clear that as soon as they understood what they were being asked to vote *on*, they wanted no part of it. Some just smiled and shook their heads; others left a little more coldly. The only person who agreed to sign was a soldier in uniform, and the male petitioner had to talk to him for at least ten minutes. It wasn't an easy sell.

I toyed with the idea of walking past the table again, just to engage in a conversation. Even after all my experiences in the battle over same-sex marriage during the last few years, I still couldn't understand why anyone would give up their Saturday to try to take someone else's rights away, especially now.

I decided to leave the mall without speaking to the couple at the table. That they were failing miserably in their attempts to get signatures was enough for me. If I've learned anything these past few years, it's that you have to choose your battles, and the "Let the People Vote" crusade was losing handily, at least in this one mall on this Saturday afternoon.

But sometimes I am drawn in. Against my better judgment, I visit websites. I read comments to stories about gay marriage posted by readers. I read entries like "Remember the good old days when alternative lifestyle cavemen were beaten to a pulp and fed to the sabertooth tigers?" I try to respond reasonably to unreasonable people. I don't know if this indicates boundless optimism or deep-rooted masochism. Perhaps it is a little of both.

During the debate on Proposition 8 in California, the referendum that ultimately took away same-sex marriage rights that had been granted by the court only six months earlier, I went online to see some of the advertisements the amendment's supporters were airing. Some were so outrageous that at first I thought the videos were *Saturday Night Live* satires. If only. The most offensive one showed a definition of marriage as one man and one woman torn apart piece by piece. Then came the images of multiple men and women all marrying, of mothers marrying sons, of men marrying children, and, the last one, of a man marrying a dog with the words MARRIAGE: 1 MAN + 1 ANIMAL. I went back to the site a few times just to verify that it wasn't a spoof. It wasn't.

The elections of November 4th, 2008, were both exhilarating and heartbreaking. I had a hard time focusing that day. I couldn't write or read, and an attempt at the gym proved just as futile. I settled in front of the television at around 5:00 p.m., shortly before Bruce came home and joined me. We ate on the sofa, trying not to become too excited when Obama picked up state after state and seemed to be on the road to the White House. Exit polling the previous two elections had burned us: We'd allowed ourselves to believe that Gore and then Kerry had won, only to be devastated by the end of the evening.

While Obama was racking up electoral votes, I was googling Proposition 8 nonstop, trying to find anything that might point to a defeat of the amendment. All I could find were predictions of a very close race, something I knew already. The first real results wouldn't come in until after eleven Eastern time.

Bruce decided to go to bed, reasonably assured Obama would win. I wish I could be more like him, able to shake off anxiety like one of our dogs shakes off water after the rain. He kissed me before he went upstairs.

"I'll find out about California in the morning," he said. "It's going to be a long night."

I agreed with him and joked that I'd wake him up if John McCain came from behind to win.

More surfing. More emails to friends.

Kate called from college just before eleven.

"Can you hear this?" she screamed over her cell phone. "It's crazy here! People are going wild!"

At eleven on the dot it happened.

Barack Obama was predicted to be President of the United States on all the networks. It was one of those moments that I knew would mark my life forever. Usually these moments are reserved for unexpected tragedies – the assassination of JFK, the explosion of the space shuttle, the September 11th attacks. Events of great joy seldom happen out of the blue, so there was no shock, no *where were you when* feeling (almost everyone was in the same place – in front of the television), but that didn't dull the emotion of the moment.

But the evening did start to dull as the results of Proposition 8 came in. Only a tiny percent of the vote had been tabulated, but we were losing already. I found a map of California on the Internet to match those cities and towns that had reported, and took comfort that the votes from the Bay area were not included.

I watched Obama's victory speech in Chicago's Grant Park. His calm and focused delivery belied the momentous nature of his election, but the thousands and thousands of weeping and cheering supporters captured the moment. I too was swept up in his words and was surprised that such a well of emotion was still in me. I gulped when he included gay people in his depiction of Americans. For so long the White House has seen us as sinners at best and evil-doers at worse.

But I couldn't stop thinking about California. I periodically checked the Proposition 8 results even as I was riveted to the news that Obama had won.

At 3:30 in the morning, I decided it was time for bed. I knew I wouldn't sleep much, but I also knew I wouldn't learn anything new no matter how long I stayed up. I spent a few hours in bed, then got up again to watch the morning news. Although we wouldn't know for sure until the end of the week, the prospects in California looked even bleaker than they did before I went to bed.

I spent the following days trying to find the silver lining to the heartbreaking loss. Yes, I knew that we did much better than the last time marriage was on the ballot out there. Yes, I knew that young people overwhelmingly supported us – an encouraging sign of things to come. And yes, I knew that more people voted with us than they did in any other referendum on marriage.

None of this really helped. But the pictures and film clips coming out of California did.

There were protests in the streets of Los Angeles, San Francisco, Palm Springs, and Long Beach. Thousands of people mobilized and would not let the issue drop. There was anger – raw, deep, and explosive – the likes of which the gay rights movement hadn't seen since Harvey Milk was assassinated thirty years earlier. I know of no other group that has ever won their rights without anger. Not one.

Anger is good.

A straight friend of mine emailed me a few days later and only half jokingly wondered where she was going to channel her anger now that the Republicans were out of power. At first it made me wonder if gay anger – directed at George Bush and the social conservatives in power for so long – would now dissipate, its focus gone. But after the Proposition 8 victory, it seemed that the gay rights movement found a focus, at least for a while: the Mormon Church. Anger over the church's involvement in passing Proposition 8 – it gave 20 million dollars to the cause and recruited thousands of foot soldiers – screamed out from the sea of homemade signs at the protest. Hoards of protesters gathered in front of Mormon temples from Salt Lake City, Utah, to Westlake, California.

I wished I could have flown out to California and been part of the demonstrations. Those of us in Massachusetts had been there, trudging down to the State House for days on end during the Constitutional Convention – a small price to pay for what we ultimately achieved in the state. We knew about legal limbo and the oppressive power of churches. I sent emails to friends and signed petitions. I was the wet blanket at the party when my straight friends hugged me saying, "Can you believe it? Obama! We did it! What an amazing time!" and I had to respond, "Yes, but…."

The week after the election Kate sent me an email letting me know that there were nationwide protests against the passage of Proposition 8 in California. Every state in the country would host at least one rally. In Massachusetts, there would be two: one in Northampton (which Kate planned to attend) and another in Boston.

I knew I needed to go. Remembering Bruce's reluctance to attend the protests in 2003 when the issue of gay marriage exploded in Massachusetts, I simply told him I was going without asking if he'd like to come, too.

"Would you mind if I joined you?" he asked.

"Mind?" I said. "I would love to go to one of these things with you. I just thought you couldn't do it."

"But we're married now," he said. "A few years ago, I didn't trust our government here in Massachusetts to let us get married. I didn't trust our federal government, either. We've been married for three years and I doubt that it's going to be an issue again in this state. And with Obama in the White House, I can't believe we'll have to worry about an amendment to the US Constitution."

If I had any doubts about why Bruce didn't want to go with me to the State House four years ago, they were completely put to rest. It really *wasn't* personal.

We drove into the Alewife Station parking lot and up to the third floor where I found a space at the end of a row. I'm a horrible parker, and Bruce reminded me of this when I turned off the car.

"Honey, you're not straight."

"Isn't that why we're going into Boston today?"

The ride in was familiar: Harvard Square, Central Square, Kendall Square, Mass General Hospital, and finally Park Street, the same stop I would get off to go to the State House. Only this time Bruce and I walked on to Government Center and Boston City Hall.

As we approached the arena-like Government Center, I was stunned when I saw the size of the crowd. Thousands of people had come to protest, many dancing to Aretha Franklin's "Respect" that blasted from the loudspeakers. Signs bobbed liked buoys in the nearby Boston Harbor, many targeting the Mormon Church for its twenty-million-dollar contribution to passing Prop 8. YOU HAVE THREE WIVES, I WANT ONE HUSBAND and SEPARATION OF CHURCH AND H8.

Bruce and I walked around the back of the crowd to get a better view of the stage that had been set up for the rally. People were ebullient. This was not the same mood I felt at the State House a few years ago, in part because no mass of counter-demonstrators tried to out-shout us. Oh, there was a sign or two in the distance that reminded us that we weren't in completely friendly territory, but these were minor blemishes on what was an extraordinarily impressive rally. A few young people wearing NO ON 8 T-shirts led us all in chants: *What do you want?* EQUAL RIGHTS! *When do you want them?* NOW!

Bruce put his arm around me. Had life ever changed. At previous protests I was shouting alone, doubting I would ever marry.

"When I was in New York," Bruce shouted in my ear over the crowd's roar, "I went to a gay pride march and the guys were yelling, *What do you want?* EQUAL RIGHTS. *When do you want them?* AFTER BRUNCH!"

I doubled over laughing.

Two members of the Massachusetts congressional delegation changed their schedules to join us and cheer us on. They pledged to keep fighting and to push Congress to repeal DOMA (Defense of Marriage Act, signed by Bill Clinton) now that we had a president who would support us. It was gratifying to see the establishment so publicly our side; not too long ago we had to convince politicians to vote their hearts and not their fears.

While most of the protest focused on California's Prop 8, three other states passed anti-gay laws on November 4th. In Arkansas, a referendum passed that now made it illegal for gay couples to adopt children. Many gay families in the state did not plan to attend the rally in Little Rock. Some gay parents believed that this new law would put their children in danger of being taken from them. I didn't know if this could actually happen, but the mere notion of its happening, of forcing gay families into hiding, should feel threatening to all Americans, not just gays and lesbians.

It began to drizzle about halfway through the demonstration, and a canopy of umbrellas opened up over the crowd. Some were appropriately rainbow-colored; others bore messages of protest. Bruce opened ours up as well, and began to shift back and forth on his feet, a sure sign that his chronic hip pain had returned. I asked him if he wanted to leave and at first he said no; after a few more suggestions that we find a place to sit down, he acquiesced. The protest was winding down anyway.

As we headed back toward the Park Street Station, we passed

about six people holding anti-gay marriage signs.

"I have an idea," I said to Bruce. I grabbed his hand, and we slowly walked past the counter-demonstrators. They looked at us and smiled; it was the *hate the sin love the sinner* expression I've come to know. But the smiles were pasted on, fake, like the mirthless laughter meant to cover up the true feelings of a very angry man. We simply kept walking.

It was one of the most quietly empowering moments I'd experienced since I'd begun my engagement in this cause.

Bruce suggested we have lunch off Tremont Street. We entered a tired old restaurant with a floor of hundreds of small hexagon tiles. A bar lined one side of the room. We sat against a wall. Bruce decided on a dish called, "Adam and Eve on a Raft." He explained that it was diner-speak for eggs (Eve) on toast (the raft) with ham (Adam).

"The least you could do is order Adam and *Steve* on a raft," I said. "We spend the morning fighting against heterosexual exclusivity and you give in to it for a few eggs and ham."

Bruce laughed, then looked at me quietly. He slowly reached for my hand across the table.

"I am so very, very, glad you're my husband," he said.

I tried to put Proposition 8 aside for a few weeks. I was fairly successful, until Barack Obama announced that Rick Warren would give the convocation at his inauguration. Warren is a vehemently anti-gay minister who has compared my relationship with my husband to incest and pedophilia. The press depicted gay reaction to Warren as a mere political difference, as if the gay community were opposing someone who simply wasn't in agreement with us on marriage. If this were the case, gay people would not have voted for Barack Obama: he, too, expressed his opposition to same-sex marriage. As had Joe Biden, Hilary Clinton, John Edwards, and virtually every other national politician in the Democratic party. No, this was about a person who saw gays and lesbians as morally inferior and who actively preached this message.

I didn't want to be angry. Not at this enormously important moment in our history. But I became even more dismayed when Obama tried to defend his choice of Warren by claiming to want all voices at the table in the name of unity. Really? What about a segregationist voice at the table? A minister who preached that women are inferior to men and should remain subservient to them in marriage? And besides, Warren hadn't been invited to a table. He'd been invited to a podium to lead the nation in prayer. This was not the road to the unity Obama claimed as his goal. Unity at the expense of dignity is not a virtue.

On the news one night, a commentator suggested that selection of Warren was a mere gesture to appease conservatives.

"Obama simply threw a bone to the right wing," he said. "It'll pay off."

I was tired of being every politician's bone. I was tired of people having to find common ground over bones.

I was probably far too outraged about this than I should have been, but it felt like the first month of the Clinton administration when, after wooing gay voters, he signed into law the "Don't Ask, Don't Tell" policy that banned openly gay Americans from serving in the military. I'd become used to being mistreated by the right wing. I really didn't want to become used to feeling the same way about Obama.

My reaction to Proposition 8 in California and to Obama's announcement that Rick Warren would lead the inauguration invocation was troubling to me. Sometimes I felt crazy. I found myself checking the news every five minutes, much the same way I did in the days leading up to the election. (The Prop 8 story continues to be in the news. As of this printing, a federal court has ruled it unconstitutional, and the issue seems to be making its way to the United States Supreme Court.)

I posted a few entries on Facebook, including one that said that I "wondered how a pastor who excludes certain Americans from entering his church is supposed to unify the country in prayer on Inauguration Day." Warren does not allow "unrepentant gays" to go to his church. Not surprising, but one more reason that Obama's decision didn't make sense to me. The idea that someone who doesn't even believe gay people exist, that my being gay is nothing more than a sum of my sins – the very idea of Obama wanting this person to speak tapped into a cynicism that I didn't think was supposed to characterize the Obama years.

I felt less crazy when I talked to my gay friends like Ed and some straight ones like Joan and Jen. Readind the blogs and watching gay reactions on television, also helped. I was not alone in this. I might have been obsessing too much, I might have let myself hit rock bottom and eat nothing but a large bag of potato chips, I might not have gone out all day. Yes, those were symptoms of a distressed soul. But as the day went on, I began to believe that the selection of Rick Warren had distressed millions of souls in this country, and that I shouldn't be too hard on myself if my particular symptoms weren't pretty.

Bruce told me he had rarely seen me so depressed as I was.

"You were eating like you were depressed," he said. "You weren't talking. Even the dogs couldn't cheer you up."

I acknowledged that I was depressed, and I began to tell him about how deeply I was affected by the Inauguration Day situation.

"I know I'm nuts," I said. "It's a five-minute prayer."

"No," Bruce said. "You are *not* nuts. I think you just expect more from Obama than he is going to give. The country hasn't changed. It's the same country where millions of people don't want us married."

"I thought my desire to move to Canada was going to lessen once Obama was in," I said.

"My desire to move hasn't changed," Bruce said.

It occurred to me that my reaction wasn't so irrational when seen in the context of growing up gay in the United States. For decades, I'd been told that gay people didn't exist. I saw no gay people either in my life or even on TV. There were no books. The Catholic Church told me that my orientation was nothing more than an urge I had to resist for my salvation, as if I were on a diet and homosexuality was ice cream. I was invisible. I had to sit through classes of teachers I knew were homophobic. (I remember one in particular telling me that I was interpreting a poem as a "faggot fantasy.") I entered adulthood full of self-doubt about my very existence.

And now, as a fifty-year-old man who trusted a politician enough to give him money and enthusiastically vote for him, I was being told that his administration would begin with words from a man who denies the very existence of gay people and who equates what I do with the most heinous of crimes.

I did have reason to be angry. But I had been angry often these past years during the battle over gay marriage. I had been outraged and euphoric. I had been confident, anxious, optimistic, frightened, deeply moved and as stubborn and steadfast as I'dever known myself to be. I had been and will be these things again. And again.

Despite my disappointment with Barack Obama, I was greatly relieved when he became president. I might not be able to trust him completely with marriage equality, but I doubt that any amendment to the Federal Constitution will have any chance of passing while he's in the White House.

Shortly before the inaugural I was on the treadmill at the gym. I was listening to a group of commentators as they sat in Washington in a pre-Inaugural telecast. Cameras were also in Maryland, where Obama and Biden boarded a train that would take them to DC the next day. One piece of the conversation went like this:

"It's amazing that Barack Obama is on a train in a state that only forty years ago didn't allow interracial marriage. And now he will become the first African American President of the United States."

"I'm forty-one. The ban on interracial marriage was overturned *in my lifetime.*"

"My very own parents had to travel to another state to get married because they couldn't get married in Virginia."

"It's amazing that in our lifetimes some states wouldn't recognize all marriages."

"It's really hard to believe, isn't it?"

Well, yes. It is hard to believe. It's hard to believe that it didn't dawn on these journalists that what they were describing is taking place today. And it's not naïve to think that someday, journalists will be in front of the cameras wondering aloud how gay couples had to move from state to state just to get married. I can hear them: *It's astonishing that this was happening in this country not that long ago.*

But it is. It is happening here. It is happening now.

And no doubt it will continue to happen here and now. Yet one of the narratives from same-sex-marriage struggle is the story of millions of Americans whose thinking is shifting on the matter. Despite the many setbacks, the mood *is* very different. People are less likely to do a double-take when I present a check bearing both our names along with the words, "We support marriage equality." We now cross the border between the United States and Canada at least ten times a year when we visit our second home in Toronto. No one has remarked on our status or questioned our relationship for quite some time.

It was in Toronto where Bruce and I met Kate's girlfriend. Kate was coming to see us during her spring break with some friends of hers. On the phone one night Kate said to me, "You'll get to meet my girlfriend." I was a little surprised by the throw-away nature of the delivery, even though Kate knew she had a receptive parent on the phone who would do nothing but support who she was.

When she arrived, girlfriend and other friends in tow, I realized she didn't really need support for being who she was. Her relationship with her girlfriend was a given. The two of them and their friends – all straight – hit the bars that night. The photos show Kate and her girlfriend dancing along with straight couples. I'm glad I didn't give her the "We're right behind you" speech. It might have been the equivalent of initiating the birds-and-the-bees talk to a twenty-year-old.

When Kate dresses up, she wears pants, shirt, and a necktie. Charlotte recently donned a blue evening gown for a formal dance. In photos they are both smiling, not only for the camera, but because they are happy. They are comfortable with who they are and who they were born to be. Their lives' work will be what to *do* with their lives rather than trying to hide who they are. Their confidence has a ripple effect. I can't help but imagine them years from now on their wedding day, each marrying not someone the government says is permissible, but someone they love. Truly love.

ACKNOWLEDGMENTS AND THANKS

This book is a memoir, not a work of research. I wrote most of the book without sources. However, much of the political information came from my daily reading of a number of newspapers and websites. Of particular importance was *The Boston Globe*. I also carefully read both the complaint by the seven plaintiff couples and the decision by the Massachusetts SJC.

A number of people supported me as I wrote this memoir, but none more than Joan Wickersham, without whose critical eye and extraordinary friendship this book could not have been written. I am also (as always) indebted to Ed Burdekin, whose belief in me as a writer had carried me this far. And there isn't a better or more compassionate editor and publisher on the planet than Jack Estes.

I am also grateful to readers of early drafts. I thank Mameve Medwed for this and so much more. Claire Cook has been the very definition of generosity. And not a day seemed to go by when Jen Tobin wasn't asking to read more of the manuscript. And when she did, her enthusiasm for the project was priceless. Thanks also my sister, who helped me remember.

I know I speak for many when I say that the seven plaintiff couples who brought their case to the court changed my life.

And, of course, not a word of this book would have been written if I hadn't met my husband.

Books from Pleasure Boat Studio: A Literary Press

Among Friends / Mary Lou Sanelli / $15 / an aequitas book
Unnecessary Talking: The Montesano Stories / Mike O'Connor / $16
Listening to the Rhino / Dr. Janet Dallett / $16 / an aequitas book
Falling Awake / Mary Lou Sanelli / $15 / an aequitas book
Way Out There: Lyrical Essays / Michael Daley / $16 / an aequitas book
Speak to the Mountain: The Tommie Waites Story / Dr. Bessie Blake /
biography / $18 / $26 / an aequitas book
Rumours: A Memoir of a British POW in WWII / Chas Mayhead / $16
The Enduring Vision of Norman Mailer / Dr. Barry H. Leeds / criticism /
$18
When History Enters the House: Essays from Central Europe / Michael
Blumenthal / $15

Orders: Pleasure Boat Studio books are available by order from your
bookstore, directly from our website, or through the following:
SPD (Small Press Distribution) Tel. 8008697553, Fax 5105240852
Partners/West Tel. 4252278486, Fax 4252042448
Baker & Taylor 8007751100, Fax 8007757480
Ingram Tel 6157935000, Fax 6152875429
Amazon.com or Barnesandnoble.com

Pleasure Boat Studio: A Literary Press
201 West 89th Street
New York, NY 10024
Tel / Fax: 8888105308
www.pleasureboatstudio.com / pleasboat@nyc.rr.com

LaVergne, TN USA
09 February 2011
215913LV00004B/135/P